PRIVACY PROGRAM MANAGEMENT

Tools for Managing Privacy Within Your Organization

(pre GDPR)

This textbook is what test is on.

Executive Editor and Contributor
Russell R. Densmore, CIPP/US, CIPP/IT
Deputy Chief Privacy Officer, Lockheed Martin Corporation

Contributors
James M. Byrne, CIPP/US, CIPP/G, CIPP/IT
Elisa Choi, CIPP/IT
Ozzie Fonseca, CIPP/US
Edward P. Yakabovicz, CIPP/IT
Amy E. Yates, CIPP/US

An IAPP Publication

Cover design: Noelle Grattan, -ing designs, llc.

Copy editor: Sue Ducharme, TextWorks

Compositor: Ed Stevens, Ed Stevens Design

Indexer: Wendy Catalano, Last Look Editorial Services

ISBN: 978-0-9885525-1-7
Library of Congress Control Number: 2012955874

About the IAPP

The International Association of Privacy Professionals (IAPP) is the largest and most comprehensive global information privacy community and resource, helping practitioners develop and advance their careers and organizations manage and protect their data.

The IAPP is a not-for-profit association founded in 2000 with a mission to define, support and improve the privacy profession globally through networking, education and certification. We are committed to providing a forum for privacy professionals to share best practices, track trends, advance privacy management issues, standardize the designations for privacy professionals, and provide education and guidance on opportunities in the field of information privacy.

The IAPP is responsible for developing and launching the first broad-based credentialing program in information privacy, the Certified Information Privacy Professional (CIPP), and the Certified Information Privacy Manager (CIPM), the first and only global certification in privacy program management. The CIPP and CIPM are the leading privacy certifications for professionals who serve the data protection, information auditing, information security, legal compliance and/or risk management needs of their organizations. Today, many thousands of professionals worldwide hold an IAPP certification.

In addition, the IAPP offers a full suite of educational and professional development services and holds annual conferences that are recognized internationally as the leading forums for the discussion and debate of issues related to privacy policy and practice.

Contents

SECTION I: Privacy Program Governance

CHAPTER ONE

Strategic Management

CHAPTER TWO

Develop and Implement a Framework

CHAPTER THREE

Performance Measurement

SECTION II: Privacy Operational Life Cycle

CHAPTER FOUR

Assess

CHAPTER FIVE

Protect

CHAPTER SIX

Sustain

CHAPTER SEVEN

Respond

Figure List

Table List

Preface

The sophistication of technology is advancing at a rapid pace. The growth of the Internet, globalization, and the potential to exploit data have driven new technologies and practices to help safeguard information. Privacy-related laws, regulations and consumer expectations are rising, and organizations must be prepared to respond in a proactive fashion to these ever-increasing challenges to data privacy management. As local legal compliance challenges evolve, the privacy professional must be prepared to assess, protect, sustain and respond to meet jurisdictional, organizational and strategic requirements placed upon every organization throughout the world that operates in a jurisdiction with privacy legislation. A structured privacy approach simplifies and demystifies privacy management by providing a comprehensive framework that allows for proactive management. Rather than reacting when an issue arises, an organization with established privacy-management best practices is better prepared to react during privacy-related incidents and breaches or when legal disputes arise.

> *The fantastic advances in the field of electronic communication constitute a greater danger to the privacy of the individual...*
>
> —*Earl Warren, 14th chief justice of the United States (1953–1969)*

The privacy management model presented in this book leverages many past and current best practices, including books, manuals, and education and training data, to build a privacy program. Specifically, this book uses the 2012 Swire and Ahmad *Foundations of Information Privacy and Data Protection: A Survey of Global Concepts, Laws and Practices* book and the 2011 Herath *Building a Privacy Program: A Practitioner's Guide* book as foundations to define privacy and the many elements that each privacy professional should know and understand for successful privacy management. This privacy management book expands on those ideas and topics to prepare the privacy professional to establish a **privacy governance model** or refine current privacy management and then to use the **privacy operational life cycle** to maintain privacy management through best practices to *assess, protect, sustain and respond* to privacy-related events.

I would like to thank all of the contributing authors, especially Ed Yakabovicz of Lockheed Martin Corporation for his significant contributions in shaping this privacy management model. Through many hours of refinement and practical application of privacy principles we have created what is intended to be a valuable tool for anyone wishing to manage a new or already established privacy program.

Russell R. Densmore, CIPP/US, CIPP/IT
December 2012

Acknowledgments

The IAPP is pleased to present *Privacy Program Management: Tools for Managing Privacy Within Your Organization* in support of our Certified Information Privacy Manager (CIPM) program.

The CIPM is the first global certification in privacy management. I am enormously grateful for the team of privacy professionals who provided their time and expertise to the development of the Body of Knowledge for this program: James M. Byrne, CIPP/US, CIPP/G, CIPP/IT, Mickey Clemons, CIPP/US, Joe Glowacki, CIPP/US, Elizabeth Lake, CIPP/US, CIPP/G, Sagi Leizerov, CIPP/US, Paresh Majethia, Frank Morgan, CIPP/US, CIPP/E, CIPP/IT, Gokul Padmanabhan, CIPP/US, Theodore Tsang, Richard Tychansky, CIPP/G and Thomas Welch.

I would also like to thank the members of our Certification Advisory Board/ Management who provided guidance and advice. These members are:

Yim Y. Chan, CIPP/C
Privacy and Data Protection Executive, IBM Corporation
Chief Privacy Officer, IBM Canada

Andrea Chard
Chief Privacy Officer, AstraZeneca

Russell R. Densmore, CIPP/US, CIPP/IT
Deputy Chief Privacy Officer, Lockheed Martin Corporation

Jonathan Fox, CIPP/US
Director of Data Privacy, McAfee, Inc.

Christine M. Frye, CIPP/US
SVP Privacy Compliance Executive, Bank of America

Timothy Mark Gough, CIPP/US, CIPP/E
Data Protection and Information Risk Manager, Guardian News and Media

Doris A. Patrick, CIPP/US, CIPP/C, CIPP/IT
Global Privacy Manager, Ally Financial

Susan Smith, CIPP/US
Privacy Officer, Americas Region, Hewlett-Packard Company

Russell R. Densmore, CIPP/US, CIPP/IT was a tremendous partner on this project as the book's executive editor. In addition to his written contributions, he managed every stage of the development of this text from chapter outlines, to initial draft, through several revisions to the final manuscript. This book would not have been possible without his professionalism and commitment.

Thank you to James M. Byrne, CIPP/US, CIPP/G, CIPP/IT, Elisa Choi, CIPP/IT, Russell R. Densmore, CIPP/US, CIPP/IT, Ozzie Fonseca, CIPP/US, Edward P. Yakabovicz, CIPP/IT and Amy E. Yates, CIPP/US who shared their knowledge and experience within the chapters in this book and to David Hare of SDG Associates who contributed his writing talents to portions of the text. I also thank Yim Y. Chan, CIPP/C, Timothy Mark Gough, CIPP/US, CIPP/E, Benjamin S. Hayes, CIPP/US, CIPP/C, CIPP/E, CIPP/G, CIPP/IT, Simon McDougall, CIPP/E, Doris A. Patrick, CIPP/US, CIPP/C, CIPP/IT, Marcus Sinha, Susan Smith, CIPP/US and Ron L. Wadey, CIPP/C who reviewed the text during its development for content and scope.

I would like to acknowledge Alfredo Della Monica, CIPP/E, Ulrika Dellrud, CIPP/E, Ellis I. Parry, Gayle Pearce, CIPP/E and Louise Thorpe, who reviewed chapters of this book and added practical sidebars to highlight key points, as well as Rachel Deschuytner who researched and validated references throughout the text. To the editorial and production team—Jocelyn Humelsine, Rebecca Mahoney, Ed Stevens and Wendy Catalano—thank you for your high-quality work and attention to detail.

I am grateful to all of these professionals who provided insight and guidance to ensure that we published a text that both helps CIPM candidates prepare to achieve their CIPM designation and serves as an indispensable resource on the field of privacy management.

Richard Soule, CIPP/US, CIPP/E
Certification Director
International Association of Privacy Professionals

Introduction

When the IAPP was created in 2000, the chief privacy officer was a somewhat obscure position—and was often a firm's only employee charged with ensuring that personal data was appropriately managed.

As the digital landscape exploded over the last decade and as news stories of privacy concerns increased, so has the need for companies to thoroughly embed sound privacy practices and information governance policies throughout the organization, from top to bottom and across departments.

The IAPP's mission has been to improve the privacy profession, and through our certification programs—CIPP/US, CIPP/C, CIPP/E, CIPP/G, CIPP/IT—we have sought to educate our members about the *"what"* of privacy. Our thousands of certified members have learned what privacy professionals need to know about existing laws, regulations, obligations and other privacy-related best practices.

Our newest certification, the Certified Information Privacy Manager (CIPM) program, expands the privacy professional's knowledge to include the *"how"* of privacy.

With the constant threat of data breaches, increased use of Big Data and the reliance on storing data in the cloud, privacy has become a competitive differentiator in the marketplace. Often the reputation of a company can be severely affected by poor information management practices. It is paramount for organizations to have a structured framework to manage data so that they are prepared to handle day-to-day issues, and more major privacy incidents. In other words, organizations increasingly need to be proactive with their data management practices and policies—not reactive.

Drawn from the expertise of Executive Editor Russell R. Densmore, CIPP/US, CIPP/IT, and the invaluable contributions of Experian's Ozzie Fonseca, CIPP/US, Avanade's Amy Yates, CIPP/US, Ernst & Young's Elisa Choi, CIPP/IT, and a host of experts from Lockheed Martin, *Privacy Program Management: Tools for Managing Privacy Within Your Organization* will help you prepare for this practical certification.

This textbook addresses two primary domains: privacy program governance and the privacy operational life cycle. The former focuses on strategic management, developing and implementing a privacy framework and performance measurement, while the latter offers insight into privacy program maintenance through four life cycle stages: assess, protect, sustain and respond.

The CIPM is the perfect tool for privacy professionals working in both the public and private sectors, but the principles and policies herein will not only serve privacy professionals but also those in adjacent professions across jurisdictions and industry sectors.

I am extremely excited about this new certification. It adds a pragmatic dimension to an already robust suite of privacy certifications. If you're just getting your organization's privacy or information governance program underway, or if you're looking to improve your already existing framework, this text and certification are for you. I applaud your efforts.

J. Trevor Hughes, CIPP
President and CEO
International Association of Privacy Professionals

PRIVACY PROGRAM GOVERNANCE

This privacy management model provides suggestions for a structured approach through two key high level tasks and supporting subtasks. This section on privacy program governance explores:

- Strategic management
- Developing and implementing a framework
- Performance measurement

The privacy operational life cycle is discussed in Section II.

CHAPTER ONE

Strategic Management

Strategic management is the first high-level task necessary to implementing proactive privacy management through three subtasks:

- Define your organization's privacy vision and privacy mission statements
- Develop privacy strategy
- Structure your privacy team

Strategic management is important to define and implement. It is needed to structure responsibilities with business goals. It ensures strategic objectives are connected to the daily operations of an organization in assigning roles, setting expectations, granting power and verifying performance. A strategic management model identifies alignment to organizational vision and defines the privacy leaders for an organization, along with the resources (people, policy, processes and procedures) necessary to execute the vision. Strategic management authorizes privacy-related decisions to include use, protection and management practices that relate to how the organization handles privacy from the executive leadership of the organization through to the day-to-day activities.

> **Key Definition**
>
> *Privacy professional. General term used to describe a member of the privacy team who may be responsible for privacy program framework development, management and reporting within an organization.*

1. Create an Organization Privacy Vision and Mission Statement

Strategic management of privacy starts by creating or updating the organization vision and mission statement based on privacy best practices that should include:

- Develop vision and mission statement objectives
- Define privacy program scope
- Identify legal and regulatory compliance challenges
- Identify organization personal information legal requirements

1.1 Develop Vision and Mission Statement Objectives

The vision or mission statement of a corporation's privacy strategy and program is critically important. This statement is the key factor that lays the groundwork for the rest of the privacy program elements. It is typically comprised of a short sentence or two that describe the purpose and ideas in less than 30 seconds. It indicates the privacy vision of the organization and includes consensus from many stakeholders to facilitate acceptance. Mission statements explain what you do as an organization, not who you are; what the organization stands for and why what you do as an organization to protect personal information is done.

> *A privacy mission statement describes the purpose and ideas in just a few sentences. It should be read in less than 30 seconds.*

Privacy can be covered in that mission statement, or a specific privacy mission statement can be created. As Herath states, "In just a few clear sentences, it communicates to stakeholders across all your different lines of business—from legal to human resources to sales and marketing—where the organization stands on privacy ... your customers and partners and the auditors and regulators with whom you deal need to feel confident that they understand how your privacy policies and procedures will affect them, that you are meeting any legal requirements and that you are protecting their interests."[1] Examples include:

Australian Bankers Association: From 21 December 2001, the ABA considers it is bound by the Privacy Act 1988 (Cth) ("Privacy Act") and the National Privacy Principles contained in the Privacy Act. Our policy is to comply with the Privacy Act, and that includes telling you about the ABA's policies for managing personal information that we may collect, hold, use or disclose for the purposes of our functions and activities.[2]

Citibank: Our goal is to maintain your trust and confidence when handling personal information about you. Our Online Privacy Statement describes how we may collect, use and share information you provide when you visit this website, receive our emails or interact with advertisements we have on third-party websites.[3]

Ireland, Office of the Data Protection Commissioner: Our Mission is to protect the individual's right to privacy by enabling people to know, and to exercise control over how their personal information is used, in accordance with the Data Protection Acts, 1988 and 2001.[4]

Hong Kong, the Office of the Privacy Commissioner for Personal Data (PCPD): Our mission is to secure the protection of privacy of the individual with respect to personal data through promotion, monitoring and supervision of compliance with the Ordinance.[5]

Hong Kong Trade Development Council (HKTDC): We respect your privacy and we promise:

- To implement computer, physical and procedural safeguards to protect the security and confidentiality of the personal data we collect
- To limit the personal data collected to the minimum required to provide a better service
- To permit only properly trained, authorized employees to access personal data
- Not to disclose your personal data to external parties unless you have agreed, we are required by law or we have previously informed you.[6]

U.S. Immigration and Customs Enforcement (ICE): The mission of the ICE Privacy Office is to sustain privacy protections and the transparency of government operations while supporting the ICE mission. The Privacy Office develops internal policies to protect personal privacy, promotes awareness of and compliance with privacy requirements and ensures that ICE technology systems have appropriate privacy protections in place.[7]

U.S. Veterans Affairs (VA): Preserve and protect the privacy of veterans and VA employees' personal information.[8]

A shared mission statement and vision is a product of many stakeholders. Thus, it has a better chance of acceptance and success because it receives greater support and less resistance to changes in privacy policies, management and direct employee actions when handling personal information. This statement should indicate:

- The value the organization places on privacy
- Desired organizational objectives
- Strategies to drive the tactics used to achieve the intended outcomes
- Clarification of roles and responsibilities

While the intended objectives may vary depending on your industry and location and the size of the organization, the core principles that guide your objectives remain constant. They should answer the primary question, "How do we assess, protect, sustain and respond to data privacy and the protection of personal information?"

1.2 Define Privacy Program Scope

In establishing the scope of the privacy program, you must first understand and identify the legal and regulatory compliance challenges of the organization and identify the data impacted. This analysis is not a linear exercise; typically, your organization is subject to many data protection laws—and some data may be subject to more than one regulation. As an example: your organization may provide health services and is subject to regulations governing the handling of personal health information. You may also handle financial transactions and therefore be subject to financial reporting regulations as well. Since no two entities are alike, you will need to determine the true scope for your particular situation.

If your organization plans to do business within a jurisdiction that has inadequate or no data protection regulations, institute your organization's requirements, policies and procedures instead of reducing them to the level of the country in which you are doing business. Choose the most restrictive policies—not the least restrictive.

Companies that span the globe will need to develop a global privacy strategy relevant to markets, cultures and geographical locations. The privacy organization must be aware of cultural norms and legal and regulatory compliance. Management practices used in one country may be alien in another in respect to the people, culture or laws. The privacy organization must:

- Understand the global perspective in order to meet legal, cultural and personal expectations
- Customize privacy approaches from both global and local perspectives
- Be aware of privacy challenges that include translations of laws and regulations, and enforcement activities and processes
- Monitor all legal compliance factors for both local and global markets

Some of these principles will be reviewed in further detail later in this book, but this serves as the starting point to clarify the difficulties in domestic and multinational privacy management, along with some of the steps to define the program scope.

1.3 Identify Legal and Regulatory Compliance Challenges

Privacy compliance is a challenge regardless of whether the program is domestic or global. Domestic programs can span state or regional laws, while global programs may span laws in various countries, cultures, languages and business methods. Identifying these challenges will be the first concern of the privacy professional, who must ensure relevant laws, regulations and other factors are considered from the start and throughout the privacy program life cycle. While most people are aware that European countries, the United States and Australia have enacted data protection laws, a significant number of other nations have also enacted some sort of data protection legislation, and many other countries are in the process of joining this list. These laws may apply to your organization whether it is located and operated in the country itself or whether your organization is located in another country (and personal information is transferred to your organization). As Baker and McKenzie state in their looking-ahead analysis of 2012, "A few important trends are taking shape.

- Data privacy is being incorporated into and serving as an anchor for much broader view of corporate compliance ... this trend will have a profound impact on the role and importance of privacy professionals within an organization.

- The goal of "achieving compliance" is steadily being replaced with a corporate need to "achieve and maintain compliance."

- We are also witnessing a strong desire on the part of global businesses to move beyond a state of "crisis management" toward more proactive strategies that aim to anticipate, prepare for, and create opportunities to share information about a potential crisis before they occur."[9]

Baker and McKenzie approach the compliance challenges this way: "Individual nations differ in their approach to privacy protection. In the United States, for example, legislators recognizing the potential harm and risk to individuals of breaches and the misuse of data have identified key sectors of civic life in which privacy protection is of special importance. For example, in the realm of healthcare, patients are made aware that medical information about them will not be disclosed, used or shared without their knowledge and/or consent. In the arena of financial transactions, laws now require consumer reporting agencies—the main source of credit ratings—to disclose the personal information they hold that influences an individual's chance to successfully apply for credit ... Differing from the United States in its approach to privacy, the

European Union (EU) has enacted broader, more comprehensive laws. The EU has established a uniform standard that is designed to ensure individual privacy protection and facilitate the free movement of personal data between member countries."[10] Table 1.1 illustrates how the philosophies differ around the globe.

Table 1.1: Sample Approaches to Privacy around the Globe

Country/ Protection Models	Approach to Privacy Protection
United States/ Sectoral Laws	Enactment of laws that specifically address a particular industry sector, such as: <ul><li>Financial transactions</li><li>Credit records</li><li>Law enforcement</li><li>Medical records</li></ul> Drawbacks include: <ul><li>Technology relevancy</li><li>Oversight through new legislation</li></ul>
European Union member states, Canada/ Comprehensive Laws	Govern the collection, use and dissemination in public and private sectors with an official oversight enforcement agency that: <ul><li>Remedies past injustices</li><li>Promote electronic commerce</li><li>Ensure consistency with Pan-European laws</li></ul> Drawbacks include: <ul><li>Varying degrees of data protection official power and varying levels of resources for enforcement that lead to inadequate funding and protection</li></ul>
Australia/ Co-Regulatory Model	Variant of the comprehensive model, where industry develops enforcement standards that are overseen by a privacy agency
United States, Japan, Singapore/ Self-Regulated Model	Companies use a code of practice by a group of companies as industry bodies; drawbacks include adequacy and enforcement. The Online Privacy Alliance (OPA), TRUSTe, BBBOnline, and WebTrust are examples of this type of model.

Domestic privacy challenges for organizations operating in the United States, for example, include an initial determination about whether your organization constitutes an entity that is subject to a law or industry standard that regulates data or the collection of data from certain individuals. "Financial institutions," as defined by the Gramm-Leach–Bliley Act (GLBA), are subject to GLBA.[11] Certain types of organizations and entities known as "covered entities," such as healthcare providers (e.g., hospitals, clinics, pharmacies) and health plans (e.g., medical plans, organization benefit plans) are subject to the Health Insurance Portability and Accountability Act of 1996 (HIPAA).[12] Websites collecting information from children under the age of thirteen are required to comply with Federal Trade Commission (FTC) Children's Online Privacy Protection Act (COPPA). A merchant of any size that handles cardholder information for debit, credit, prepaid, e-purse, ATM and POS cards must be in compliance with the Payment Card Industry Data Security Standard (PCI DSS), which is a global standard. As is obvious from the name, PCI DSS is an industry security standard, not a law, but it still imposes certain data protection requirements on organizations, as well as certain notification obligations in the event of breaches; some U.S. states have adopted PCI DSS as part of legislated requirements. Domestic U.S. challenges also extend from federal laws and regulations to the local states; up to 46 states now have data breach notification laws.[13] Accordingly, if you process the personal information of any resident of a state that has adopted a breach notification law, understand that to the extent that non-encrypted data has been compromised, your compliance obligations may include notification to the residents of the states, as well as government bodies or state attorney general offices.

It is worth adding that in many countries the government may be subject to other or more stringent laws than private sectors businesses. For example, in Europe, you will be subject to the national data protection legislation of all countries in which you process personal data, so you will need to understand the requirements of, and differences in, data protection law in each member state. There are also separate requirements for sectors such as telecommunications providers in relation to record-keeping. Government bodies may be subject to higher levels of scrutiny than the private sector. Many other countries follow the EU model. There are also industry-specific laws in countries like Japan and Australia.

As shown, the challenges to legal and regulatory compliance within complexity, cultural norms, relevant markets and geographies span the globe. There is no one linear approach. Instead, the organization privacy scope within legal and regulatory compliance challenges must be understood and translated to align to the organization objective and goals to ensure complete and successful data privacy management.

1.4 Identify Organization Personal Information Legal Requirements

The first step in gaining assurance that you are complying with your regulatory obligations is to know what personal information your organization holds and how it uses it. There are a number of ways to ascertain this. Some organizations engage an outside consultancy to assess where personal information is collected, stored, used and shared. Other organizations engage their own internal audit or privacy team resources. If your organization elects to take a less structured approach to identifying data and legal requirements, it can still start "roughing out" the scope of a privacy program by flagging areas in an organization where personal information is likely to be collected, accessed or used. In most organizations, these areas include human resources, finance, marketing, and

IT/IS (information security). It is also common for personal information to be stored in marketing and customer relationship management systems. If your organization delivers services to customers or consumers that involve the processing of personal information, then these areas of your business must be examined. You will also need to understand any marketing laws that work in conjunction with privacy legislation. For example, in the United Kingdom, the Privacy and Electronic Communications Regulations contain privacy rules for any form of electronic marketing, in addition to a vast array of statutes, regulations and voluntary codes of practice that govern direct marketing activity.[14]

The privacy office must understand the legal requirements that affect the organization through the constant changing of domestic and international privacy laws. As laws are developed, changed or retired, the privacy office should be prepared to interpret and adjust the organizational practices. Any organization operating around the globe must be prepared for the legal requirements concerning the proper handling of personal information, which can be substantial and complex. For these very reasons, the privacy office must plan and organize activities within a framework for the organization to operate and function.

Specific questions that should be asked to determine the privacy legal requirements include:

- Who collects, uses, and maintains personal information relating to customers and employees? This includes your service providers in addition to your own legal entity, so you need to understand these relationships too.
- What are the types of personal information and what are the legal requirements for that data? For example, healthcare information, banking, etc.
- Where is the data stored physically?
- When is the data collected? For example, during a transaction or hiring process.
- How is the data collected?
- Why is the information collected?

Another six key questions to ask include:

1. Who is covered by the laws?
2. What type of information is covered?
3. What exactly is required or prohibited?
4. Who enforces the law?
5. What happens if we don't comply?
6. Why does the law exist?

Many other factors can also be considered when determining the legal aspects of privacy management, which will be covered in Chapter 2.

2. Develop a Privacy Strategy

Developing a privacy strategy, no matter the industry or the size of the organization, can be a complex and challenging task. Personal information may be collected and used across an organization, with many individuals responsible for protecting this information. No one solution mitigates all privacy risk, and there is no "one-size-fits-all" strategy that can be adopted. The good thing about implementing a privacy strategy in today's environment is there is a growing awareness among management about the importance of protecting personal information, and there could be a financial impact if mismanaged. Even so, developing a vision and implementing a solution can still be difficult.

Building a privacy strategy may mean changing the mind-set and perspective of an entire organization. Effectively protecting personal information within an organization requires every member of the organization to do his or her share. This means that management needs to approve funding to resource and equip your privacy team, fund important privacy enhancing resources and technologies, support privacy initiatives such as training and awareness, and hold employees accountable for following privacy policies and procedures. Sales personnel must secure business contact data and respect the choices of these individuals. Software developers must incorporate effective security controls, build safe websites, and create solutions that require the collection or use of only that data necessary to accomplish the purpose. All staff must understand and employ the fundamental practices required to protect personal data—from secure methods to collect, store and transmit personal data (both hard copy and electronic) through to secure methods of destruction. Everyone in an organization has a role to play in protecting the personal information that an organization collects, uses and discloses. The adage "The chain is only as strong as its weakest link" truly reflects how an organization must approach its privacy program. There are no shortcuts, and every individual within an organization contributes to the success of a program.

Before your organization can embark on this journey, your management team will need to understand why their involvement and support is so critical. It is important to know your ultimate destination before you begin and to have a roadmap for the journey. These factors and more must be contained in the privacy strategy to ensure success, buy-in and ownership from the widest possible pool of stakeholders. This section will detail the data necessary to develop and define the organizational privacy strategy. Other sections of the book will add greater detail for each of these steps.

2.1 Identify Stakeholders and Internal Partnerships

One of the most challenging aspects of building a privacy program and the necessary supporting strategy is building a consensus among the members of your organization's management that a business imperative exists. You must build this consensus in stages.

Your first major goal in building your coalition of supporters is to conduct informal one-on-one conversations with executives within your organization who have accountability for information management and/or security, risk, compliance or legal decisions. Internal partners, such as human resources (HR), legal, security, marketing, risk management and IT, should also be included in conversations, as they too will have ownership of privacy activities, and their buy-in will be necessary. Depending on your organization's industry and business, the corporate culture of your organization and the personalities of the various members of your management team, the executives, managers and internal partners will each play some role in the development and implementation of your privacy strategy into the privacy program.

Out of these communications, you should start to get a feel for which executive, or if an executive is even necessary, will serve as the program sponsor, or "champion," for the privacy program. The program sponsor should be someone who understands the importance of privacy and will act as an advocate for you and for the program. Effective program sponsors typically have experience with the organization, the respect of their colleagues and access to or ownership of budget. Final budgetary decision makers are the best program sponsors, but if they are unavailable, it is best to obtain approval from executive management closest to the organization's top executive. Frequently, sponsors function as risk or compliance executives within the organization. Sometimes chief operating officers or chief information officers serve as program sponsors.

> *A privacy champion at the executive level acts as an advocate and sponsor to further foster privacy as a core organization concept.*

Most organizations, regardless of their size, industry and specific business, use personal information for roughly the same bundle of activities—for example, staff recruitment and ongoing employment administration, customer relationship management and marketing, order fulfillment, etc. Further, the use of this personal information is managed by a similar array of executives—regardless of the organization or its activities. It is common to call the individual executives who lead and "own" the responsibility of the relevant activities "stakeholders." Typically in a larger organization, an executive privacy team will be comprised of some or all of the following individuals: senior security executive (e.g., chief security officer, CSO), senior risk executive (e.g., chief risk officer, CRO), senior compliance executive (e.g., chief compliance officer, CCO), senior human resources executive, senior legal executive (e.g., general counsel), senior information executive (e.g., chief information officer, CIO), senior physical security/business continuity executive, senior marketing executive, and a senior representative of the business.

Several best practices when developing internal partnerships include:

- Become aware of how others treat and view personal information
- Understand their use of the data in a business context
- Assist with building privacy requirements into their ongoing projects to help reduce risk
- Offer to help staff meet their objectives while offering solutions to reduce risk of personal information exposure
- Invite staff to be a part of the privacy advocate group to further privacy best practices

2.2 Leverage Key Functions

Managing privacy within an organization requires the contribution and participation of many members of that organization. Because privacy should continue to develop and mature over time within your organization, functional groups must understand just how they contribute and support the overall privacy program, as well as the privacy principles themselves. Importantly, individual groups must have a fundamental understanding of data privacy because, in addition to supporting the vision and plan of the privacy officer and the privacy organization, these groups may need to support independent initiatives and projects from other stakeholders. In some larger organizations you might find that members of the privacy team sit within other functional groups and have a dedicated privacy role—for example, a marketing privacy manager may advise and sign off on new marketing initiatives and e-mail campaigns from a privacy perspective. He or she may report to both the senior marketing manager and the head of privacy. Buy-in and a sense of ownership from key functions also assist with better acceptance of privacy and sharing the mission of the responsibility across the organization rather than in one office. Based on the individual culture, politics and protocols of the organization, the privacy professional will need to determine the best methods, style and practices to work within the organization. In the long run, this effort may be onerous, but afterwards the bonds and relationships will be much stronger and better understood.

There are many functions that directly support the various activities required by the privacy program. Among these activities are the adoption of privacy policies and procedures, development of privacy training and communications, deployment of privacy and security-enhancing controls, contracting with and management of third parties who process the personal information of the organization, and the assessment of compliance with regulation and established control mechanisms.

As a rule, privacy policies and procedures are created and enforced at a functional level. Policies imposing general obligations on employees may reside with ethics, legal and compliance; HR policies and procedures that dictate certain privacy and security requirements on employees as they relate to the technical infrastructure typically sit with

IT. Policies that govern requirements that need to be imposed on provider of third-party services that implicate personal data typically sit with procurement. Policies that govern the use and disclosure of health information about employees of the organization typically reside with HR. Since activities that contribute to the protection of employee, customer and other data subjects' personal information span the entire organization, most groups within the organization should have some policies to address the appropriate use and protection of personal information specific to their own functional area; all such policies will need to be produced in close consultation with the privacy office. There needs to be an awareness of the difference between having appropriate policies in place and whether appropriate controls are actually being used. These include:

- Training and awareness—with the intention of changing bad behaviors and reinforcing good ones—are integral to the success of the privacy program. Many organizations have a learning and development group that manages activities related to employee training. This function enables policies and procedures to be translated into teachable content and can help contextualize privacy principles into tangible operations and processes. In smaller companies these responsibilities may fall upon the privacy function. Whatever the size of the organization you work for, the privacy team will always need to approve the training output that has been produced.

- The communications group can assist with publishing periodic intranet content, e-mail communications, posters and other collateral that reinforce good privacy practices.

- The information security (IS) group is more closely aligned to the privacy group than any other function in the organization. One can safely say that every security-enhancing technology that IS deploys—from encryption, to parameter security controls, to data leakage prevention (DLP) tools—help the privacy program meet its requirements to implement security controls to protect personal information. As an example, EU data protection law incorporates security provisions into the law as one of its key principles. The IS group ensures that appropriate technological controls are employed (e.g., complex passwords, encryption, role-based access) and whether the various groups within an organization are aware of, and comply with, the organizational and technical controls that govern their activities and behaviors.

- The information technology (IT) group supports and enhances the effectiveness of the privacy program by adding process and controls that support privacy principles. For example, creating processes to develop and test software and applications in a manner that does not require the use of production data decreases the chances that the data will be compromised and that individuals who have no business need will access the data. Creating systems that support role-based access also supports the larger purposes of the privacy program by specifically identifying and limiting who can access the personal information in a particular database. The IT group should carry the mantle of "privacy by design" by implementing privacy principles into the realm of technology development—such as limiting the data fields that are built into a tool or application to only those actually required to perform a process or action, or building in functions that enable the user to easily delete data according to a retention schedule.

- One could consider an internal audit group an ally of the privacy program and, in a sense, a member of the privacy program, although it traditionally functions independently to assess whether controls are in place to protect personal information and whether people and processes within the organization are abiding by these controls.

- Procurement plays an important role in ensuring that contracts are in place with third-party services providers who process personal information on behalf of the organization and that the appropriate data privacy contractual language is imposed on these service providers. Most privacy laws require data controllers or other entities directly subject to data protection laws to ensure their privacy requirements are fulfilled. You must perform due diligence, action the results, and have the right contractual clauses to reduce your exposure.

In smaller organizations, a legal department may actually create contract requirements if there is no procurement.

2.3 Create a Process for Interfacing Within an Organization

Protecting personal data and building a program that drives privacy principles into the organization cannot be the exclusive job of the privacy officer or the privacy team, any more than playing a symphony is the exclusive responsibility of the conductor. As with an orchestra, many people, functions and talents will merge to execute on a vision.

Many organizations create a privacy committee or council comprised of the same stakeholders (or representatives of functions) that were identified at the start of the privacy program implementation process. Just as these same individuals and functions will be used to get the privacy program off the ground, their expertise and involvement will continue to be tapped as remediation needs are identified—some of which may sit within their areas of responsibility. They will be instrumental in making strategic decisions and driving such strategies and decisions through their own organizations.

Organizations with a global footprint often create a governance structure that is comprised of representatives from each geographic region and business function (i.e., legal/ HR) in which the organization has a presence to ensure that proposed privacy policies, processes, and solutions align with local laws (and to nuance them where necessary).

Herath states this concept another way by saying the privacy professional must become part of the business solution, not an inhibitor. This involves interfacing closely with colleagues in many capacities across the organization as both an advisor and advocate. He states, "Expertise will help staff in other functions meet the privacy requirements of your organizational policy and applicable laws and regulations. Your ability to advocate and be proactive will help float privacy as an important, valuable, and ongoing consideration in many of the organization's internal groups."[15]

2.4 Develop a Data-governance Strategy for Personal Information (Collection, Authorized Use, Access, Security, Destruction)

Taking an inventory of relevant regulations that apply to your business will enable you to create a data-governance strategy for your organization. Once you have determined which laws apply, you must design a manageable approach to handling and protecting this information. It will be nearly impossible to successfully implement and manage a program designed to address the various rights and obligations of each privacy regulation on a one-off basis. One option to consider is to take a more pragmatic approach and collect the various data-protection requirements and "rationalize" them where you can. Rationalizing requirements means implementing a solution that materially addresses the various requirements of the majority of laws or regulations with which you must comply. This activity is made simpler by a number of factors. First, at a high level, most data privacy legislation imposes many of the same types of obligations on regulated entities, and much of this regulation requires entities to offer similar types of rights to individuals. Among these shared obligations and rights, data-protection regulations typically include: notice, choice, consent, purpose limitations, limits on retaining data, individual rights to access, correction and deletion of data and the obligation to safeguard data. Further, there seems to be a growing consensus among data-protection regulators and businesses about which actions and activities meet these regulatory obligations.

Following a rationalized approach to creating a privacy strategy also requires addressing those requirements that fall outside of the common solution when the risk of not creating a specific solution for a particular set of requirements is too great, or the effort to implement and manage these specific requirements are trivial.

Typically, organizations include language respecting how they, as employers, collect, use and protect the personal information of their employees' personal data when they provide offer or employment letters. It is prudent to start with a very clear and concise statement about the processing of this data. After you have created a type of notice from which you can build, you should work with local counsel to ensure that there are no local data protection laws that require the inclusion of any verbiage or other content specific to that region.

In contrast, if you are deploying a global performance management tool that collects data from employees and is accessed by all employees through the organization's intranet, it might be difficult to create separate and distinct online notices that would be nuanced to specifically address employees on a country-by-country basis. In this instance, one would post a notice that provides information about the processing of the personal data collected, stored and accessed on that site in a manner that materially addresses the common notice criteria of all of the various data protection regulations, with country-specific supplements.

Another activity that lends itself to establishing a standard process that meets the requirements of many countries but may require some "customization" to meet local requirements is the granting of access to personal data to individuals and the timeframes within which that the data must be provided to them. In EU countries, there may be prescribed timeframes within which an organization must provide access to individuals (e.g., employees, consumers). They may be different country by country. In countries where no legal requirements exist (and the granting of access may merely be an organization policy), or where there is a generous amount of time extended to provide data, the organization can adopt a procedure that sets a common time period within which data must be provided. However, in certain countries with more stringent access requirements, such as those with the self-regulating models, it is likely that individual procedures must be adopted to ensure the organization in that geographic location is able to act in a manner consistent with local data-protection requirements.

Technical security controls are also part of the data-governance strategy and are often a privacy area where technology-based solutions are routinely deployed. The good news is that most legislation does not enumerate the types of specific controls that must be implemented to protect personal data. Security controls also have similar categories and solutions designed to protect the confidentiality, integrity and availability of the data; thus, the technical security controls that one deploys in one jurisdiction may typically satisfy another jurisdiction. The privacy professional should always involve a security engineer to review, define or establish technical security controls, including common security controls such as firewalls, malware anti-virus, and complex password requirements. Even with technical security safeguards, it is important to become educated about local requirements and/or local prohibitions. Some countries, like China, will not permit the use of encryption, and many EU countries limit the use of data leakage prevention technology, because they interpret it to be employee monitoring. In sum, technical security controls afford the most opportunity to deploy personal information protection techniques in a uniform manner. Technical security controls will be further addressed later in this book.

One last strategy that many organizations employ is, when possible, to look to the strictest standard when seeking a solution; provided that it does not violate any data privacy laws, exceed budgetary restrictions or contradict organization goals and objectives. This approach is used more frequently than most organizations realize—for example, rather than instructing employees they only need to shred documents that contain personal information or confidential information, organizations may implement a "shred everything" policy. Organizations may roll out laptop encryption for the entire employee population as opposed to only targeting those individuals who may perform functions that involve personal information.

In summary, crafting a comprehensive personal information protection strategy may not result in a one-size-fits-all solution. Instead, one must look at the various activities an organization performs and the obligations that must be discharged and attempt to create a common solution for the various activities and privacy requirements. Based on an assessment of cost, risk, legal regulations and implementation complexity, the organization must determine whether to apply a common solution to a particular activity or safeguard, or create a one-off solution.

2.5 Conducting a Privacy Workshop for Your Stakeholders

With the support of the privacy program sponsor, you should plan to conduct a workshop for those stakeholders who will support efforts to develop and launch a privacy program. Don't assume that everyone in the room has the same level of understanding about the regulatory environment or the complexity of the undertaking. There will invariably be different levels of privacy knowledge among your various stakeholders. This is your opportunity to ensure everyone has the same baseline understanding of the risks and challenges your organization faces, the data privacy obligations that are imposed on your organization and the increasing expectations in the marketplace regarding the protection of personal information.

Conduct a privacy workshop for your stakeholders to level the privacy playing field by defining privacy for the organization, explaining the market expectations, answering questions, and reducing confusion.

3. Structure the Privacy Team

Structuring the privacy team is the last objective to formalizing the organization's approach to privacy. This section will focus on the many factors that should be considered by the privacy professional to assist with the decisions to structure the privacy team and ensure the foundation for those decisions align to the business objectives and goals. This last step helps to determine privacy governance for the organization to align to the privacy strategy.

3.1 Governance Models

There are many different opinions and strategies for creating privacy office governance models. This text is not intended to educate thoroughly on the idiosyncrasies of various governance models but to give examples of types of governance models you may wish to consider when structuring your privacy program. You should give this issue consideration, as it will help identify what decisions your privacy team are relied on to make and the policies they will need to establish.

You should consider whether or not the model applies only within a given region(s) or whether your team should globally consider your operations. Many large organizations find they need to consider those global implications when structuring the privacy team.

The positioning of the privacy team should also consider the authority it will receive based on the governance model it follows. Positioning the privacy team under the corporate legal umbrella may be substantially different from aligning the team under the IT umbrella. Executive leadership support for your governance model will have a direct impact on the level of success when implementing your privacy strategies.

No matter which model you choose, there are some important steps to integrate into it:

- Involve senior leadership
- Involve stakeholders
- Develop internal partnerships
- Provide flexibility
- Leverage communications
- Leverage collaboration

Privacy governance models include centralized, local and hybrid versions but are not limited to only these selections. Governance models and the choice of the correct model objectives should ensure information is controlled and distributed to the right decision makers. Since decision making must be based on accurate and up-to-date management data, the allocation and design of the governance model will ensure intelligent and accurate decisions.

3.1.1 Centralized

Centralized governance is a common model that fits well in organizations used to utilizing single-channel functions (where the direction flows from a single source) with planning and decision making completed by one group. A centralized model will leave one team or person responsible for privacy-related affairs. All other persons or organizations will flow through this single point. Often this single point is the chief privacy officer or corporate privacy office.

3.1.2 Local or Decentralized

Decentralization is the policy of delegating decision-making authority down to the lower levels in an organization, relatively away from and lower than a central authority. A decentralized organization shows fewer tiers in the organizational structure, wider span of control, and a bottom-to-top flow of decision making and flow of ideas.

In a more decentralized organization, the top executives delegate much of their decision-making authority to lower tiers of the organizational structure. As a correlation, the organization is likely to run on less-rigid policies and wider spans of control among each officer of the organization. The wider spans of control also reduce the number of tiers within the organization, giving its structure a flat appearance. One advantage of this structure, if the correct controls are in place, will be the bottom-to-top flow of information, allowing decisions about lower-tier operations to be well informed. For example, if an experienced technician at the lowest tier of an organization knows how to increase the efficiency of production, the bottom-to-top flow of information can allow this knowledge to pass up to the executive officers.

3.1.3 Hybrid

A hybrid governance model allows for a combination of centralized and local governance. This is most typically seen when a large organization assigns a main individual (or organization) responsibility for privacy-related affairs and for issuing policies and directives to the rest of the organization. The local entities then fulfill and support the policies and directives from the central governing body. Members of the privacy team may also sit locally; for example, with regional compliance hubs in large multinationals. Each region may have a privacy manager who reports in to local management and/or the chief privacy officer at the global level.

3.1.4 Centralized, Decentralized and Hybrid

Centralized management offers many advantages, with streamlined processes and procedures. This allows the organization to create efficiency by using the same resources throughout the organization. Since decisions are made at the top layer, individual employees or groups cannot make their own decisions and must seek approval from a higher level.

With fewer layers of management, decentralized managers create and manage their own business practices. This may be inefficient because each process may be reproduced many times instead of using one centralized process. Employees are also tasked with solving problems to which they are closest and familiar.

The hybrid approach uses a decentralized decision-making process that tends to provide less outside influence for employees, yet offers the advantage of the organizational resources of a larger, centralized organization. Typically, the hybrid model will dictate core values and let the employee decide the practice to use to obtain those goals. Working groups, individual offices and other groups are encouraged to make business decisions to include revenue, operating costs and operations. These types of models allow an organization to function in a global environment yet remain an organization with common missions, values and goals.

Mixing centralized and decentralized management approaches into a hybrid approach allows the organization to achieve desired results that may span the globe or locations across town. Employees feel their contributions provide a sense of ownership, which encourages the employees to perform more efficiently and effectively, consistent with top management.

3.2 Establish the Organizational Model, Responsibilities and Reporting Structure Appropriate to the Size of the Organization

In establishing the overall organizational privacy model, one must consider the organizational structure as related to strategy, operations and management for responsibilities and reporting. The privacy professional should know how each major unit functions and understand their privacy needs. The following is a short list of those offices for both large and small organizational structures, including:

- Chief privacy officer
- Privacy manager
- Privacy analysts
- Business line privacy leaders
- "First responders," incident response and security computer incident response team
- Data protection officers (including those for whom privacy is not their only responsibility)

Organizational structures function within a framework by which the organization communicates, develops goals and objectives, and operates daily. Companies can use one of several structures or switch from one to another based on need. Principals within that framework allow the organization to maintain the structure and develop the processes necessary to do so efficiently. Methods and processes to consider include:

- **Hierarchy of command.** The authority of senior management, leaders and the executive team to establish the trail of responsibility
- **Role definition.** Clear definition of the responsibilities to create individual expectations and performance
- **Evaluating outcomes.** Methods to determine strengths and weaknesses and how to correct or amplify as necessary
- **Altering organizational structure.** Remain dynamic and change as necessary to meet current objectives, adopt new technology, or react to competition

- **Significance.** Large organizations typically use complex structures, while smaller organizations use flat structures
- **Types of structures.** Product organizational structures, functional organizational structures and others
- **Customers.** Consider the customer base based on products and services offered
- **Benefits.** To the organization, customers and stakeholders, as aligned to the objectives and goals
- **Considerations.** For centralized, decentralized or hybrid approach

3.3 Establish/Endorse the Measurement of Professional Competency

Privacy certifications for the privacy organization should be considered in order to train professionals on the most current and relevant privacy practices. As required by the EU EC 45/2001,[16] privacy training and certification after an appointment is mandated to develop skills and maintain proficiencies. Certifications, in general, should be considered a best practice to information privacy program development, structure and management as related to regulatory compliance and laws, as well as international concerns. A certification designation, such as those offered by the International Association of Privacy Professionals (IAPP), identifies the individual as having achieved a fundamental understanding of privacy laws, concepts, technologies and practices that are integral to information management as established by reputable third-party organizations.

Conferences and seminars can be rich sources of information and expert suggestions on effective ways to build a privacy program and address privacy governance. An individual may learn about various approaches from privacy professionals by attending presentations or panel discussions that are assembled specifically to address this topic. Often, a person learns about various governance structures and approaches to privacy through presentations on other topics. Managing security incidents, creating a sustainable training and awareness program, designing and implementing programs or other presentations on privacy challenges can inform the audience on the topic itself while also providing insights into how an organization manages these issues and assigns accountability. Information can also be obtained through informal exchanges of ideas. Most privacy professionals are engaged in some phase of rolling out a privacy program launch—the challenging thing about privacy is that technologies always change, new laws are always adopted and processes can always be improved. Learning from your peers is an incredibly valuable method for acquiring information about privacy approaches.

4. Summary

Developing a privacy strategy can be a complex and challenging task. Using a strategic management model assures that an organization's approach to privacy is in alignment with business objectives and goals. It defines both the privacy leaders of an organization and the people, policies, processes and procedures needed for the organization to meet these objectives.

Endnotes

1 Kirk M. Herath, *Building a Privacy Program: A Practitioner's Guide*, 73. Portsmouth, NH; International Association of Privacy Professionals: 2011.

2 Australian Bankers' Association, *Privacy Policy*, www.bankers.asn.au/Privacy-Policy.

3 Citibank, URL: https://online.citibank.com/JRS/portal/template.do?ID=Privacy.

4 Data Protection Commissioner, *Mission Statement*, www.dataprotection.ie/ViewDoc.asp?fn=/documents/about/1b.htm&CatID=61&m=a.

5 Office of the Privacy Commissioner for Personal Data, Hong Kong, *The Role of the PCPD*, www.pcpd.org.hk/english/about/role.html.

6 Hong Kong Trade Development Council (HKTDC), www.hktdc.com/mis/pps/en/Privacy-Policy-Statement.html.

7 ICE, Privacy Office, *Mission Statement*, www.ice.gov/contact/privacy/.

8 United States Department of Veterans Affairs, *VA Privacy Service*, www.privacy.va.gov/.

9 Baker & McKenzie. *Global Privacy Handbook Supplement*, 1 (IAPP 2012).

10 Herath, *Building a Privacy Program*, 17.

11 Gramm-Leach-Bliley Act, 15 U.S.C, Subchapter I, § 6809 (1999).

12 45 C.F.R. §§ 160.102, 160.103.

13 National Conference of State Legislatures, *State Security Breach Notification Laws*, www.ncsl.org/issues-research/telecom/security-breach-notification-laws.aspx.

14 The Privacy and Electronic Communications (EC Directive) Regulations 2003, www.legislation.gov.uk/uksi/2003/2426/contents/made.

15 Herath, *Building a Privacy Program*, 116.

16 http://eur-lex.europa.eu/LexUriServ/LexUriServ.do?uri=CONSLEG:2001R0045:20010201:EN:PDF or http://ec.europa.eu/stages/information/privacy_en.htm.

CHAPTER TWO

Develop and Implement a Framework

The term *privacy* has varying definitions and uses among nations, states, regions and industries. These definitions, while usually similar, can be vastly different. Most agree that privacy is not the same as secrecy and thus should not be confused with data classification models used by the governments of the world, who may label information as sensitive, secret, top secret, etc. Privacy is a dynamic object with a discrete set of attributes and actions that is difficult to observe and measure; therefore the use of a privacy framework provides the guidance necessary to ensure a successful program implementation.

Key Definition

Privacy program framework. An implementation roadmap that provides the structure or checklists (documented privacy procedures and processes) to guide the privacy professional through privacy management and prompts them for the details to determine all privacy-relevant decisions for the organization.

Since privacy is a subject of global importance, organizations can no longer ignore the requirements necessary to protect personal information imposed by law, relevant regulations and industry best practices. As governments are imposing tighter laws and regulations, consumers continue to demand more protection, and social networking increases, privacy management is becoming increasingly more important. Consequently, information technology (IT) organizations must meet these demands through placement of greater controls, processes and procedures on information under their custodial control. With so many spheres of influence and pressure, the privacy team must now track, manage and monitor the dynamic changes that appear to occur daily.

> *Privacy framework is an important tool in encouraging the development of appropriate information privacy protections and ensuring the free flow of information...*
>
> — *Asia-Pacific Economic Cooperation (APEC), 2005*[1]

As shown with all business management tasks, a privacy governance framework provides the methods to access, protect, sustain and respond to the positive and negative effects of all influencing factors. This master plan, or framework, thereby provides reusable procedures and checklists that outline the operational life cycle courses of action, research and subject matter expertise, constituting a "best practice" approach to an idea, thought or subject. Like maps, frameworks provide inquiry topics and direction (e.g., problem definition, purpose, literature review, methodology, data collection and analysis) to ensure quality through repeatable steps throughout program management, thereby reducing errors or gaps in knowledge or experience. For the purpose of this book, this framework is called the "privacy program framework." Although the privacy team owns this framework, it shares ownership and management aspects with other stakeholders throughout the organization, including employees, executive leadership and managers, and external entities such as partners, vendors, other third parties and even customers.

> *Framework benefits: Reduce risk; avoid incident of data loss; sustain organization market value and reputation and provide measurement in compliance to laws, regulations and standards.*

1. Frameworks

Effective privacy programs reduce the privacy risk of data management, protecting against accidental disclosures and breaches, and in so doing reduce the chance that the enterprise or its staff or customers will suffer financial or reputational harm. Effective privacy programs also can serve as competitive advantages by reflecting the value the organization places on the protection of personal information, thereby deserving trust. Because the selection of the correct privacy regulations, policies, controls and other factors is complex and difficult, organizations can make use of an objective-based privacy program framework to assist in data privacy management, personal information protection and solutions to privacy issues. The business benefits of an effective, reusable framework are significant and include:

- Lowering risk solutions
- Avoiding an incident of data loss
- Sustaining market value and reputation
- Supporting business commitment and objectives to stakeholders, customers, partners and vendors

- Complying with laws, regulations and industry standards

Simply put, frameworks provide the structure and implementation roadmap to guide the privacy professional through privacy management activities that prompt them for the details to determine the privacy-relevant decisions for the organization.

There is no one-size-fits-all privacy standard; thus, a privacy program framework provides the necessary information and design patterns to build an effective privacy program. It allows an adaptable and flexible approach to assist in making strategic business decisions in the selection of methods, strategy and technologies applicable to the protection of personal information and to privacy concerns for data usage today. This provides the architectural guidance and framework to associate current privacy standards and practices to that of data privacy protection within business objectives and goals.

1.1 Current Privacy Frameworks

Privacy frameworks began emerging in the 1970s, and today there are many choices based on geographical, political and national boundaries. Examples include:

- **The APEC Privacy Framework.**[2] A framework to enable regional data transfers to benefit consumers, businesses, and governments.

- **Guidance from local data protection authorities.** Such as the United Kingdom's (UK) Information Commissioner's Office or France's Commission nationale de l'informatique et des libertés (CNIL).

- The **Canadian Personal Information Protection and Electronic Documents Act (PIPEDA) principles**[3] and **Australian Information Privacy Principles.**[4] provide a well-developed and current example for generic privacy principles implemented in a national law.

- The **Organisation for Economic Co-operation and Development (OECD) Privacy Guidelines.**[5] The most widely accepted privacy principles; together with the Council of Europe's Treaty 108, they provide the basis for the European Data Protection Directive.

- **Privacy by Design.** Solutions are built by organizations to ensure consumers' privacy protections at every stage in developing their products. These include reasonable security for consumer data, limited collection and retention of such data, and reasonable procedures to promote data accuracy.

- **U.S. Government.** The White House privacy framework for protecting privacy and promoting innovation in the global digital economy.[6]

- **U.S. Government.** Federal Trade Commission (FTC) recommendations for business and policymakers.[7]

The differences between each will not be addressed in this book, but it can be said they each have varying objectives, based on business needs, commercial grouping, legal/

regulatory aspects, government affiliations, etc. Instead, certain aspects of each will be generalized in this chapter to help the privacy professional create a tailored privacy program framework for his or her organization. The framework that will be developed will be representative of a high-level "system design" that meets the business objectives of the organization, thus teaching the privacy professional those steps necessary to develop an open, more dynamic process to manage the specific organization needs, rather than use static frameworks that become quickly dated and are not adaptable to the organization. Regardless of laws, regulations or standards throughout the world, the privacy program framework outlined herein will allow the privacy professional to perform these tasks in a dynamic and flexible structure.

A framework answers primary privacy questions that include:

1. Are privacy and the organization's privacy risks properly defined and identified in the organization with a business case?

2. Has the organization assigned responsibility and accountability for managing a privacy program?

3. Does the organization understand any gaps in privacy management?

4. Does the organization monitor privacy management?

5. Are employees properly trained?

6. Does the organization follow industry best practices for data inventories, risk assessments and Privacy Impact Assessments?

7. Does the organization have an incident response plan?

8. Does the organization communicate privacy-related matters and update that material as needed?

This privacy operational life cycle ensures the organization is prepared to assess, protect, sustain and respond within the context of the ever-changing privacy demands of the world. Using the privacy policy framework in conjunction with the privacy operational life cycle thereby allows "*quick wins*" and *long-term* privacy management efforts that ensure accurate, complete and successful coverage of key privacy topics affecting the organization, stakeholders, consumers and customers.

Highlighting the potential costs of not having a privacy policy framework—fines, reputational damage, loss of earnings—can help gain management buy-in.

2. Develop Organizational Privacy Policies, Standards and/or Guidelines

The steps identified to create the privacy policy framework are not necessarily conducted in a rigid order, and not every organization will perform every phase. The process is flexible and further enhanced through allowable "tailoring," which should be accomplished early and with forethought and diligence. Specifically, it should focus on the rigor with which events are conducted and documented, rather than the wholesale disregard of any specific activity. Teams are cautioned against cutting out or truncating activities based solely on the lack of time or resources. For example, for very large organizations, every phase should be completed to ensure the highest accuracy in the selection and definition of privacy definitions and drivers. A smaller organization may choose to do one, some or all tasks. A highly detailed formal analysis may not be necessary, and many of the phases many need only a quick review. The execution of these events may not need to be as formal or as time-consuming, based on organizational needs.

A smaller organization may select to do one, some, all or none of these tasks.

The first step of this process includes an assessment of the ***business case*** for the current (or forthcoming) privacy program or privacy requirements for privacy policies, standards and/or guidelines. A ***gap analysis*** of this information follows, ensuring there are no gaps or holes in the current privacy program or in the development of a new privacy program. Final steps are to ***review and monitor*** the program and then ***communicate the framework***. These phases are not necessarily conducted in a rigid order, and not every organization will perform every phase.

No matter the size of the organization, if the core business of the organization revolves around the processing of personal data, having in place as thorough a privacy framework as possible becomes all the more important and should be prioritized within the organization.

2.1 The Business Case

The **business case** is the starting point for assessing the needs of the privacy organization. It defines the individual program needs and the ways to meet specific business goals, such as compliance with privacy laws or regulations, industry frameworks, customer requirements and other considerations. This allows for the understanding of the role of privacy in the context of business requirements and identification of business benefits and risks. This should be completed at a high level; the lower level detail will be examined in greater detail in the next steps.

After defining privacy and the business case, the privacy domain should be established, which will determine the privacy elements, such as industry, privacy organizations and other data, that will provide the necessary laws, standards, guidelines and other factors that should be evaluated.[8] To help assist with *business case development,* this book identifies ten foundational elements. These include selection of appropriate *privacy drivers* necessary to correctly determine the privacy needs and requirements of the organization. These elements assist the privacy professional in reviewing possible factors that impact the business case in providing a complete privacy solution.

A basic definition of each element is provided below:

- **Organizational privacy office guidance.** If developed, offers the best starting point. This should be the first step, regardless of the program maturity.

- **Define privacy.** As related to your program or organization. Use all available resources to determine the correct and appropriate definition of privacy for your organization.

- **Laws and regulations.** Provide the *mandatory government policy* and guidance based on the organization's location and industry. Well-known examples in the United States include Health Insurance Portability and Accountability Act (HIPAA), Gramm-Leach-Bliley Act (GLBA), and Privacy Act of 1974. Non-U.S. laws include Australian Privacy Act 1988 and the European Union (EU) Data Protection Directive, which is implemented in national EU laws, such as the UK Data Protection Act 1998.

- **Technical controls.** Provide the *assurances* necessary to achieve the goals of physical and data security, as well as others.

- **External privacy organizations.** Serve as *guardians* or *protectors* against misuse, loss or illegal practices. The Center for Democracy and Technology, for example, serves as a civil liberties group with expertise in law, technology and policy.[9]

- **Industry frameworks.** Provide *taxonomies* or *privacy categorization guidelines* that are not law- or regulation-based. Examples include the International Organization for Standardization (ISO), which defines itself as a non-governmental organization that has the ability to set standards that often become law, and the AICPA/CICA Generally Accepted Privacy Principles (GAPP).

- **Privacy-enhancing technologies (PETs).** Define privacy technology standards developed solely to be used for the transmission, storage and use of privacy data. Examples include Platform for Privacy Preferences (P3P) and Enterprise Privacy Authorization Language (EPAL).

- **Information technology cutting-edge or innovation solutions.** Involve the use of newer or unregulated technology, such as social networking and the new Internet web cookie policy for eGov 2.0.[10]

- **Education and awareness.** Provide methods to inform the employee of the important aspects of privacy and basic protections a non-privacy profession should know.
- **Program assurance or the governance structure.** Mandate operational safeguards that include auditing.

Organizational privacy office guidance, defining privacy, understanding applicable laws and regulations, the use of technical controls, and providing education and awareness should be prioritized—especially in smaller organizations, where resources may be scarce.

2.1.1 Element 1: Organization Privacy Office/Program/Management

If there is no privacy office or team, assemble a team of privacy professionals/ associates that will perform the work and identify stakeholders—this may be one person or many people, depending on the organization size. The privacy professional or privacy team will be the subject matter expert(s) in privacy management, while the stakeholders may consist of one or many senior leader(s) who provide strong knowledge of the business requirements and mission, strong understanding of the organization's culture and political environment, and authority to implement the solution. The stakeholders may also provide the necessary leadership and support to accomplish the **governance structure** required to approve, manage and authorize the privacy program.

Senior, local and functional top leadership endorsement and buy-in for the privacy function is necessary, especially in a smaller organization, in order to have a working privacy department and to be able to accomplish and drive the set strategies and tasks.

Assembling the team also includes these items reviewed in Chapter 1:
- Develop scope and charter
- Develop a privacy strategy
- Align your business
- Finalize operational business case for privacy
- Identify stakeholders
- Leverage key functions
- Create a process for interfacing within an organization

Finding the right people with the right skills is difficult in any situation. The privacy professional will need to combine the team talents with consideration for qualities, team structure, privacy organization structure and division for international offices, as necessary. Privacy team assembly should consider:

- Funding and other resources
- Team structure
- Skills and knowledge
- Career paths available or if those jobs must be created
- Education and certifications

2.1.1.1 Internal Policy Compliance

The privacy office should know and understand the internal policy of the organization as the key stakeholder for privacy. Key aspects of internal policy compliance include a formal written policy and designated points of contact (privacy owners) responsible to the organization for all privacy-related matters.

Written policy should document the principles, policies and practices that influence privacy for the organization. These will define the organizational and enterprise privacy principles and provide direction to the organization and employees through such documents as organization privacy practices; privacy roles and responsibilities; breach or incident documents, and others that define privacy ownership and assign stakeholders. They should also provide formal procedures for receiving and resolving privacy-related inquires and complaints from both internal and external sources.

A designated point of contact for privacy issues should also be established, such as a privacy office or privacy officer. This contact can also serve as the liaison to information security, legal and human resources, all of which are highly important partners in successful privacy management. There are additional ideas for establishing ways to contact and/or work with the privacy organization in Chapter 7 of this book.

The privacy function is not a stand-alone function. It is imperative that the privacy professional works closely with the IT, security, HR and legal functions in order to take a coordinated approach to solutions.

The bigger and more global the organization, the more important it is to have privacy resources spread out in various regions to ensure consistency and compliance. Even smaller companies would benefit from having regional (e.g., European) internal privacy contact persons (even if not on a full-time basis) who can perform some of the basic tasks of a working privacy department. By conducting regular calls on topical privacy and data protection issues and providing internal and external updates relevant to the country, the privacy professional would then create a loose network for an internal privacy office.

Apart from having the necessary privacy policies and procedures in place, it is equally important to actually roll them out and communicate them to the appropriate persons and have them easily accessible, which is not always the case. By way of example, a well-written employee data protection policy could certainly serve as a notice to the individuals about how the organization processes the individual's data.

> *Set up a dedicated e-mail address for all privacy enquiries, both internal and external, which the privacy team can monitor (e.g., privacy@yourorganization.com).*

2.1.1.2 Data Inventories, Risk Assessments and Privacy Impact Statements

How do you know where your personal data resides, how it is used in the organization and why it is important? The data inventory, also known as a record of authority, provides this answer by identifying the data as it moves across various systems and thus how data is shared and organized and its locations. That data is then categorized by subject area, which identifies inconsistent data versions, enabling identification and mitigation of data disparities. This then identifies the most and least valuable data and how it is accessed, used and stored.

Based on these aspects, the data inventory offers a good starting point for the privacy team to prioritize resources, efforts, risk assessments and current policy in response to incidents. A data inventory should include the items in Table 2.1.

Table 2.1: Elements of a Data Inventory

Element	Purpose
The nature of a repository of privacy-related information	Provides context and describes the purpose of the repository
The owner of the repository	A starting point for further investigation into the repository, if needed
Location of the repository	Geographical location of the data to identify where it is moving from and to
The volume of information in this repository	How much data is actually in the repository?
The format of the information	Is this a paper or electronic repository? Is it structured or unstructured?
The use of the information	How is the information being used?
Type (or types) of privacy-related information in the repository	What kinds of information are in the repository (e.g., physical or e-mail addresses, government-issued identification numbers, health information, salary information)?
Where the data is stored	In which country/countries is the data stored?
Where the data is accessed	From which country/countries is the data accessed?
International transfers	Where will the data flow (country to country)?

Once the data inventory is completed and documented, the information will be used when necessary to address both incidents and standard risk assessments. This process will help set the organizational priorities for privacy initiatives by providing data locations, data use, data storage and data access. Knowing this allows the privacy team to justify priorities and understand the scope of data usage in the organization.

> *The new proposed rules in the draft EU Data Protection Regulation will make it even more important for companies, small and large; to have a good overview of its data inventory, as security breach notification will become mandatory for all types of companies (not just telecommunications companies).*

2.1.2 Element 2: Defining Privacy for the Organization

Each organization may be subject to a different combination of laws, regulations and other mandates related to protecting the privacy of data, so as the first step, the term *privacy* should be defined for the organization to ensure a clear and concise definition, which will reduce confusion later. The privacy professional's starting point is to identify the terms *personal information* and *personal data* as associated with data use, storage and transport in the organization. These terms are interchangeable and relate to information concerning an "identified or identifiable person." As Baker and Matyjaszewski state, "All countries employ some variation of the phrasing, data 'that allow the identification of a person directly or indirectly.'"[11]

"Despite this general similarity, laws differ in what actually qualifies for data protection. Some countries list specific examples of what can constitute personal data; others are satisfied with a more flexible—or ambiguous—definition."[12] The privacy professional must first define privacy for the organization as associated with all personal information or personal data that relate to mandated compliance factors. Table 1.1 in Chapter 1 provides examples of privacy data laws around the globe.

> *Decide whether you still need the data. If you do, is it stored in the right place? If you have data you need to keep for archive purposes but do not need to access it regularly, move it to more secure offline storage. If you do not need the data, you should delete it.*

2.1.2.1 Establish the Current Baseline

Establishing the current baseline is the process of collecting "*as-is*" data privacy requirements in order to document the current environment and any protections, policies and procedures currently deployed. Review of the business case elements will assist with this process. Most of this task represents a data collection and documentation effort for current privacy management in order to generate a baseline, or starting point. This baseline will be used later on to evaluate progress as related to building the architecture. Start by collecting information on the organization's current compliance polices related to privacy, regulations, standards and security that include:[13]

- **Collection Limitation.** There should be limits to the collection of personal data and any such data should be obtained by lawful and fair means and, where appropriate, with the knowledge or consent of the data subject.

- **Data Quality.** Personal data should be relevant to the purposes for which they are to be used, and, to the extent necessary for those purposes, should be accurate, complete and kept up-to-date.

- **Purpose Specification.** The purposes for which personal data are collected should be specified not later than at the time of data collection and the subsequent use limited to the fulfilment of those purposes or such others as are not incompatible with those purposes and as are specified on each occasion of change of purpose.

- **Use Limitation.** Personal data should not be disclosed, made available or otherwise used for purposes other than those specified, except with the consent of the data subject or by the authority of law.

- **Security Safeguards.** Personal data should be protected by reasonable security safeguards against such risks as loss or unauthorized access, destruction, use, modification or disclosure of data.

- **Openness.** There should be a general policy of openness about developments, practices and policies with respect to personal data. Means should be readily available to establish the existence and nature of personal data, and the main purposes of their use, as well as the identity and usual residence of the data controller.

- **Individual Participation.** An individual should have the right: (a) to obtain from a data controller, or otherwise, confirmation of whether or not the data controller has data relating to him; (b) to have communicated to him, data relating to him within a reasonable time; at a charge, if any, that is not excessive; in a reasonable manner; and in a form that is readily intelligible to him; (c) to be given reasons if a request made under subparagraphs (a) and (b) is denied, and to be able to challenge such denial; and (d) to challenge data relating to him and, if the challenge is successful, to have the data erased, rectified, completed, or amended.

- **Accountability.** A data controller should be accountable for complying with measures which give effect to the principles stated above.

> *Consider how valuable, sensitive or confidential the personal information is and what damage or distress could be caused to individuals if there was a security breach; use that as a baseline for assessing your privacy program.*

Since privacy is much broader than just protecting the confidentiality of personal information, this effort may take longer than planned. All aspects of the current use and protection of personal information must be assembled in order to understand or assess current data privacy protections. Document all findings along the way for a historical record and to create a library of material that can be referenced. The most difficult challenge in this task is collecting sufficient detail or current documents because some organization records management systems do not collect enough information on its privacy practices. Determine up front what the key systems, applications and processes are in your organization and use this information in your initial information-gathering process. The organization's data inventory can serve as a tool to more quickly identify this information. The team should not dwell on this task in a futile attempt to find documents or practices that do not exist—make your best effort without expending excessive budget or time.[14]

2.1.2.2 Other Considerations: Privacy Domains

Also consider the privacy domains that may include the following categories. These define unique privacy identifiers the privacy professional should understand and know to include:

- **Personal Information (PI)** is from the public sector: security and privacy files that uniquely identify, contact or locate a single person, including national ID, date of birth, street addresses, driver's license, telephone numbers, Internet protocol (IP) addresses, vehicle registration, etc. As already mentioned, the term used for PI and how it is defined will change on a country-by-country basis. For example, PI is generally known as "personal data" in Europe. Argentina's Law for the Protection of Personal Data (LPPD) also calls PI "personal data" (in translation) and has a broad definition of personal data, similar to the EU Data Protection Directive, where personal data can be anything that identifies a person and could include even basic information such as name and a means of contact. Both Argentina and the EU also have a category of personal data called "sensitive personal data" (SPD), including information on racial and ethnic origin, political opinion, religious beliefs, and so on. SPD requires additional conditions to be met to process this type of data, and generally (but not always) will require a greater level of protection than personal data.

- **Non-Public Information (NPI)** is from the private sector, where government regulations may not apply, and typically includes financial application data, account histories, customer status, names, addresses, telephone numbers, Social Security numbers, PINs, passwords, account numbers, salaries, medical information and balances.

- **Protected Health Information (PHI)** is from the U.S. health sector: specifically, healthcare exemptions not made for PI in the other categories as related to transmission of health data and electronic maintenance of health data. It excludes education records covered by Family Educational Rights and Privacy Act and employment records held by a covered entity.

Each of these is grouped based on the privacy industry, custom, obligation, regulation, sector or requirement. Of these privacy domains, **personal information and personal data are the most common terms and in most cases are typically used in conjunction with the word privacy.** Regardless of the privacy domain or the definition of privacy for the organization, the privacy professional must always remember that **personal information will generally be defined as information about or associated with an individual**. Some personal information will be sensitive, while some is not considered sensitive when viewed as a **single attribute**. As already mentioned, in Europe, sensitive personal data is a subset of personal data.

2.1.3 Element 3: Laws and Regulations

This privacy element is a highly complex array of hundreds of laws, regulations and statutes. Most are based on a bottom-up approach[15] that spans public and private sectors. Since there are many laws and regulations throughout the world, you may need the assistance of the organization's legal office or a third-party research firm to ensure all relevant laws and regulations have been captured.

A spreadsheet including all of the countries within an organization's operations mapped to applicable laws and regulations for data processing can serve as a quick reference guide. The Data Protection Authorities page on the IAPP website is a good resource for this information.[16]

Using the data from Element 2 that defined privacy and the privacy domain, the privacy professional can then start the potentially onerous task of researching laws, regulations and policies in an attempt to gather all that apply. The privacy professional or the organization's legal office must understand applicable national laws and regulations, as well as local laws and regulations. Laws are typically grouped into the following categories:

- General privacy laws (e.g. EU Data Protection Directive, national privacy laws in countries such as Australia, New Zealand, Argentina, Israel and Uruguay)
- Health privacy laws

- Financial privacy laws
- Online privacy laws
- Communication privacy laws
- Information privacy laws
- Privacy in one's home

2.1.3.1 U.S. Federal Laws Governing Privacy

Table 2.2 includes the primary privacy-related laws enacted and enforced by the U.S. Federal Government:[17]

Table 2.2: U.S. Federal Privacy Laws

U.S. Federal Legislation	Agency Responsible
Gramm-Leach-Bliley Act of 1999 (GLBA)	Consumer Financial Protection Bureau (CFPB), state departments of insurance and attorneys general (see next table for more details)
Health Insurance Portability and Accountability Act (HIPAA) of 1996	Department of Health and Human Services (DHHS), Office of Civil Liberties and state attorneys general (SAGs)
Controlling the Assault of Non-Solicited Pornography and Marketing Act (CAN-SPAM) of 2003	FTC
Children's Online Privacy Protection Act of 1998 (COPPA)	FTC
Fair and Accurate Credit Transactions Act of 2003 (FACTA)	FTC and CFPB
Fair Credit Reporting Act (FCRA) of 1970	FTC and CFPB
Telemarketing Sales Rule (TSR)	FTC and SAGs
National Do Not Call Registry	FTC
Telephone Consumer Protection Act (TCPA) of 1991	FTC, Federal Communications Commission (FCC) and states
Driver's Privacy Protection Act (DPPA) of 1994	Private right of action (trial bar)
Electronic Communications Privacy Act (ECPA) of 1986	Law enforcement
Federal Trade Commission Act (Section 5: Privacy and Security) of 1914	FTC

2.1.3.2 International Privacy Laws

Various international and country-specific laws may also apply to the organization. As an example, many U.S.-based companies may do business with European countries; thus the EU Data Protection Directive must be considered to include:[18]

Table 2.3: International Privacy Laws

International Legislation	Agency Responsible
Organisation for Economic Co-operation and Development (OECD) legal guidelines for privacy protection and trans-border flow of personal data	Voluntary compliance with guidelines
EU Data Protection Directive	Country-specific supervisory authority
Australia	Office of the Australian Information Commissioner
Japan	Public Management Ministry
Canada–Personal Information Protection and Electronic Documents Act (PIPEDA) of 2000	Office of the Privacy Commissioner of Canada (Note: Canadian provinces have their own, often stricter, laws)
Asia-Pacific Economic Cooperation (APEC) privacy framework	Voluntary compliance with guidelines

2.1.3.3 Self-Regulation: Industry Standards and Codes of Conduct

In addition to U.S. laws, there are also sector-specific voluntary and contractual initiatives that establish codes of conduct for the communities of interest. Table 2.4 highlights some of the more notable self-regulatory programs.

Table 2.4: Self-Regulatory Privacy Standards

Self-Regulation (Voluntary)	Sectors Affected
Payment Card Industry Data Security Standard (PCI DSS)	All organizations (worldwide) that collect, process, store or transmit cardholder information from any card branded with the logo of one of the credit card brands
Direct Marketing Association (DMA) Privacy Promise	Businesses interested in interactive and database marketing
VeriSign and TRUSTe	E-commerce entities wishing to meet recognized industry privacy requirements
Children's Advertising Review Unit (CARU) guidelines	Media advertising to children below the age of 12
Network Advertising Initiative (NAI) guidelines	Online advertising, particularly targeting or behavioral, that potentially harms individuals

2.1.3.4 Understand Penalties for Non-Compliance with Laws and Regulations

Legal and regulatory penalties are typically imposed within any industry to enforce behavior modification due to previous neglect and lack of proper protection of data. Privacy is no different; organizations are now held accountable to protect the privacy of the data with which they have been entrusted. As penalties for violation of privacy laws and regulations become more serious, the privacy professional must be prepared to address, track and understand any penalty that could affect the organization. For example, per the U.S. Health Information Technology for Economic and Clinical Health (HITECH) Act that amended the HIPAA Privacy and Security Rules, the maximum penalty for breach of healthcare patient information is now $1.5 million.[19] Fines, as well as criminal penalties, can be imposed on the violating institution and the individuals involved. In another example, remedies for violation of the U.S. Privacy Act include a $5,000 maximum fine per record that includes civil and criminal penalties.[20] In the EU, the data protection regulations allow the authorities to fine up to £500,000 for security breaches or for failing to comply with the provisions of the regulations.[21]

This activity can be linked to the business case development but may also be accomplished after the privacy program framework has been completed. For many organizations, however, the level of fines and enforcement activity in a given jurisdiction will often guide the organization in making the priorities for remediation of its data protection compliance following a gap analysis. Therefore, it may be important to also link this activity to the business case development at the outset.

Use examples of high-profile breaches by organizations to gain management buy-in for the budget for the privacy framework.

2.1.3.5 Understand the Scope and Authority of Oversight Agencies (e.g., Data Protection Supervisory Authorities, Privacy Commissioners, Federal Trade Commission, Etc.)

Oversight typically relates to the "watchful care, management or supervision" of something. Specific to the previous section, oversight agencies can fine or impose penalties, civil and criminal, based on laws and regulations. Knowing these details is worthwhile to understanding when involvement is warranted or unwarranted, who to call or contact, and when those actions are necessary by law.

Several oversight organizations exist throughout the world, including:

- *Data Protection Authorities* **within the EU.** "Include the key actors for effective data protection. They serve as low threshold access points to effective data protection for citizens and other persons. They function as one-stop shops for all data protection concerns of citizens and other persons; including areas which were formerly part of the third pillar of the EU ... All EU Member States, in compliance with the requirements of Article 28(1) (1) of the Data Protection Directive, have conferred one national supervisory Authority with the wide remit of monitoring the application of and ensuring respect for data protection legislation within their territories. Several Member States (e.g. Austria, Netherlands) have designated one Data Protection Authority of general competence and several other sector-specific supervisory bodies (for instance, in health, post or telecommunications). Some of those States organized along federal lines or with significant powers held at the regional level (e.g. Germany, Spain) are endowed, in turn, with one national supervisory body and several sub-state agencies entrusted with the same function at the regional or federal level. Furthermore, whereas in many countries (e.g. Romania), prior to the establishment of Data Protection Authorities, the duty to monitor the respect for privacy rights was entrusted to Ombudsman institutions, in some Member States (e.g. Finland), the Ombudsman still maintains a relevant function in protecting personal data."[22]

- *Office of the Privacy Commissioner for Personal Data* (PCPD), Hong Kong. An independent statutory body set up to oversee the enforcement of the Personal Data (Privacy) Ordinance (Cap. 486) ("the Ordinance") which came into force on December 20, 1996, and updated with the provisions of the Personal Data (Privacy) (Amendment) Ordinance 2012. Their mission is to secure the protection of privacy of the individual with respect to personal data through promotion, monitoring and supervision of compliance with the Ordinance.[23]

- **The *Privacy Commissioner of Canada*.** A special ombudsman and an officer of parliament who reports directly to the House of Commons and the Senate. The privacy commissioner has the authority to investigate complaints filed by Canadian citizens and report on whether there has been a violation of the Privacy Act, which deals with personal information held by the government of Canada, or the Personal Information Protection and Electronic Documents Act (PIPEDA), which deals with personal information held in the private sector. The privacy commissioner also has the power to audit, publish information about personal information-handling practices in the public and private sector, conduct research into privacy issues and promote awareness and understanding of privacy issues by the public.

- **The United States'** *Federal Trade Commission* has three principle groups relevant to privacy oversight:
    - The Bureau of Consumer Protection protects consumers against deceptive and or unfair business practices. Included under the FTC

mandate are deceptive advertising and fraudulent product and/or service claims.

- The Bureau of Competition investigates and attempts the prevention of anticompetitive business practices, such as monopolies, price fixing and similar regulatory violations, which may negatively affect commercial competition. Criminal violations in these areas are handled by the Antitrust Division of the U.S. Department of Justice, which cooperates with the Bureau of Competition.

- The Bureau of Economics works in accord with the Bureau of Competition to study the economic effects of FTC lawmaking initiatives and of existing law. In the matter of mergers and acquisitions in critical industries, such as communications, for example, a merger that eventuates in restraint of trade or monopolistic pricing can have a major impact on the economy.

2.1.3.6 Other Privacy-Related Matters to Consider

The framework presented in these chapters covers many of the main privacy topics but not every detail for every country, state or local government. Instead, the framework provides the high-level detail necessary to manage and keep informed on privacy-relevant matters that concern any organization. Other privacy matters to consider include the geographical location, global privacy functions and organizations, and international data sharing.

2.1.3.7 Monitoring Regulations

As Nicole V. Crain and W. Mark Crain state in "The Regulation Tax Keeps Growing," the impact of regulations on business compliance throughout the world has been substantial, with cost estimates ranging from $800 billion to in the trillions of dollars over the last 10 years. They further state that in the United States alone, in 2008, the annual cost of federal regulations increased more than $1.75 trillion.[24] A 2009 U.S. OMB report estimates the cost of major federal regulations ranges between $51 billion and $60 billion.[25] As regulations continue to grow each year, and the costs to comply grow even greater, organizations must monitor and adapt to reduce risk by ensuring gaps are recognized and mitigated quickly.

As Statenet comments, "Although regulatory agencies generally provide some period of time for organizations to comply with new rules, that lead time isn't always sufficient to allow smooth implementation of mandated changes. Active monitoring of regulatory activity allows companies additional time to prepare for those changes and the various direct and indirect costs that will be incurred ... Monitoring state and federal regulatory activity is a complicated task. On top of the sheer volume—

some 30,000 measures proposed annually—there is so much variation among the nearly 6,000 state and federal regulatory agencies, state to state and even department to department, that determining which measures will actually impact a particular organization can be extremely time-consuming."[26]

Methods to track the changes include using many resources, such as the Internet, printed and online journals, automated online services and third-party vendors. Each organization should investigate the best methods based on cost, requirements and industry to ensure issue customization, easy access, professional support, reliability rating and complete, accurate coverage. Regardless of an organization's size and complexity, the privacy professional may wish to consider some form of third-party support because of the number of new laws, changing regulations and other complex factors influencing privacy today.

2.1.3.8 Third-Party External Privacy Resources

If an organization is small, or the privacy office staffing is limited, the privacy professional and organization could consider third-party solutions to track and monitor privacy laws relating to the business. These third parties include legal and consultancy services that can assign people to the organization and use automated online services that allow research on privacy law, news and business tools. Privacy professionals from large and small firms can also take advantage of a growing number of free resources to help them to keep up to date with developments in privacy. These include the IAPP's e-newsletter, *The Daily Dashboard*. Most law firms with privacy practices also regularly produce updates and often host free-to-attend seminars or webinars.

> *Each organization should determine the best methods for staying on top of relevant privacy developments, given limited resources and budgets. If the organization is small, or the privacy office staff is limited, the privacy professional and the organization could consider third-party solutions to track and monitor privacy laws relating to the business; e.g., secondment from a law firm. There are also a number of free resources to help keep up to date with developments in privacy (free webcasts, free newsletters or law firm alerts).*

As the 2012 IAPP "Privacy Professionals Role, Function and Salary Survey" report says, "In-house corporate and government privacy professionals most frequently turn to attorneys for outside advice; they rely on outside privacy consultants half as often. There are differences among regions; Americans and Europeans rely most on attorneys for outside advice, while Canadians have a more equal distribution between privacy attorneys and privacy consultants."[27] Table 2.5 reflects the results of that 2012 survey for external third-party support.

Table 2.5: Sources of Outside Privacy Support

Source	2011 #	2011 %	2012 #	2012 %
Use a privacy attorney	431	81%	377	81%
Use a privacy consultant	225	42%	184	40%
Use other privacy services firms	142	27%	130	28%

Table 2.6: Sources of External Privacy Support by Region

	U.S.	Canada	Europe	Asia-Pacific	Latin America	Middle East & Africa
Use a privacy attorney	55%	49%	58%	50%	-	100%
Use a privacy consultant	25%	40%	27%	50%	-	-
Use other privacy services firms	20%	11%	15%	-	-	-

2.1.4 Element 4: Technical and Physical Controls

Technical and physical controls are provided across the many elements of an organization, from the IT systems to employee background checks, building physical security, clean desk policy, shredders and others that are driven by laws, regulations, industry standards, geography or location. Although not typically a part of the business case, these controls should still be evaluated at a high level when defining the business case to define, explain and document these facts. Since both are cumbersome, it is highly recommended the privacy professional use subject matter experts who know and understand the complicated nature of both.

> ***Technical and physical controls*** *are driven by laws, regulations, privacy groups, industry frameworks and others. They use technology and physical protections to achieve integrity, confidentiality, availability, accountability and control of the people, processes and technology for privacy, security and others.*

One stakeholder, typically the person with oversight of information security and physical security, or others should know and understand enough to assist the privacy professional whenever an issue, question or topic arises. Controls change all the time, based on newer releases of technology, software applications, upgrades, decommissions and rotation in staff, so controls will be an agenda item at many privacy meetings to communicate, understand and provide proper management practices.

> *Develop a Privacy Impact Assessment (PIA) with IS/IT and other functions for all new systems and processes in the organization and embed it in to the organizations project management framework.*

2.1.4.1 ISO/IEC 27001

ISO/IEC 27001:2005: *Information technology—Security techniques—Information security management systems—Requirements,* more commonly known as ISO 27001, is a specification for an information security management system (ISMS). It was published in 2005 by the International Organization for Standardization (ISO) and the International Electrotechnical Commission (IEC). The United Kingdom Information Commissioner's guidance has included the use of ISO 27001 as the benchmark for due diligence on data processors.

ISO 27001 and ISO 27002 (*Information technology—Security techniques—Code of practice for information security management*) contain global standards and require that management:[28]

- Systematically examine the organization's information security risks, taking account of the threats, vulnerabilities, and impacts
- Design and implement a coherent and comprehensive suite of information security controls and/or other forms of risk treatment (such as risk avoidance or risk transfer) to address those risks that are deemed unacceptable
- Adopt an overarching management process to ensure that the information security controls continue to meet the organization's information security needs on an ongoing basis

While other sets of information security controls may potentially be used within an ISO 27001 information security management system (ISMS) as well as, or even instead of, ISO 27002, these two standards are normally used together in practice. The governing principle behind ISMS is that an organization should design, implement and maintain a coherent set of policies, processes and systems to manage risks to its information assets, thus ensuring acceptable levels of information security risk. ISO 27002 is aligned to security policies that address both technical and physical controls that include:[29]

- Security organization
- Asset classification and control
- Personnel security
- Physical and environmental security
- Communications and operations management
- Access control

- System development and maintenance
- Business continuity management
- Compliance

It is important to note that it is rare for a whole organization to be certified ISO 27001 compliant; the certification is usually limited to particular processing activities, systems or premises.

> *For smaller organizations in particular that are not ISO 27001 certified, it is key to have a layered approach to effective security, combining a number of different tools and techniques as there is no single tool or approach that will provide a 100 percent guarantee of security for an organization.*

2.1.4.2 Payment Card Industry (PCI) Data Security Standard

The Payment Card Industry Data Security Standard (PCI DSS) is an example of a standard with focus on the purely technical controls of a system to provide data security. It provides 12 security control requirements for the financial industry that apply to all system components that are included in or connected to the credit cardholder data environment. These requirements are identified in Table 2.7.

Table 2.7: PCI DSS Requirements

Category	Requirements
Build and Maintain a Secure Network	Requirement 1: Install and maintain a firewall configuration to protect cardholder data. Requirement 2: Do not use vendor-supplied defaults for system passwords and other security parameters.
Protect Cardholder Data	Requirement 3: Protect stored cardholder data. Requirement 4: Encrypt transmission of cardholder data across open, public networks.
Maintain a Vulnerability Management Program	Requirement 5: Use and regularly update anti-virus software. Requirement 6: Develop and maintain secure systems and applications.
Implement Strong Access Control Measure	Requirement 7: Restrict access to cardholder data by business need to know. Requirement 8: Assign a unique ID to each person with computer access. Requirement 9: Restrict physical access to cardholder data.
Regularly Monitor and Test Networks	Requirement 10: Track and monitor all access to network resources and cardholder data. Requirement 11: Regularly test security systems and processes.
Maintain an Information Security Policy	Requirement 12: Maintain a policy that addresses information security.

2.1.5 Element 5: Privacy Organizations

Several independent organizations have emerged over the last several years to provide sound privacy practices based on privacy issues that continue to arise worldwide. These are not government organizations but private groups formed to approach and promote privacy through sound practices. Some accomplish the task as related to human rights, while others are attuned to business needs. Regardless, they provide a common benefit of non-government information and resources to the privacy topic that would otherwise not exist at all. Some of these groups are not privacy-specific, while others were created as privacy advocates. Examples of key privacy organizations are listed in Table 2.8, which should be used as a guide within this privacy element.

Table 2.8: Privacy Organizations

American Civil Liberties Union (ACLU) www.aclu.org	Per the ACLU's web page, "The ACLU is our nation's guardian of liberty, working daily in courts, legislatures and communities to defend and preserve the individual rights and liberties that the Constitution and laws of the United States guarantee everyone in this country." These rights include First Amendment rights, equal protection under the law, right of due process and right to privacy. Specifically, the right to privacy is freedom from unwarranted government intrusion into personal and private affairs.[30]
Better Business Bureau Online www.bbbonline.org	Better Business Bureau site contains a lot of information on promoting trust and confidence on the Internet.
Electronic Frontier Foundation (EFF) www.eff.org	EFF is a nonprofit, non-partisan organization working in the public interest to protect fundamental civil liberties, including privacy and freedom of expression, in the arena of computers and the Internet. EFF was founded in 1990 and is based in San Francisco, California, with offices in Washington, DC, and New York City.
Electronic Privacy Information Center (EPIC) www.epic.org	EPIC is a public-interest research center in Washington, DC. It was established in 1994 to focus public attention on emerging civil liberties issues and to protect privacy, the First Amendment and constitutional values. EPIC is a project of the Fund for Constitutional Government. EPIC works in association with Privacy International, an international human rights group based in London, UK, and is also a member of the Global Internet Liberty Campaign, the Internet Free Expression Alliance, the Internet Privacy Coalition and the Trans Atlantic Consumer Dialogue (TACD).
Center for Democracy and Technology (CDT) www.cdt.org	The CDT covers many issues related to technology, including data privacy. CDT co-developed an informational Internet site, consumerprivacyguide.org.

Global Internet Liberty Campaign http://www.gilc.org/	The Global Internet Liberty Campaign was formed at the annual meeting of the Internet Society in Montreal. Members of the coalition include the American Civil Liberties Union, the Electronic Privacy Information Center, Human Rights Watch, the Internet Society, Privacy International, the Association des Utilisateurs d'Internet, and other civil liberties and human rights organizations.
Internet Free Expression Alliance (IFEA) http://www.ifea.net/	The name says it all. The IFEA is a consortium of organizations, such as the American Booksellers Foundation for Free Expression, the American Civil Liberties Union and the Electronic Frontier Foundation, devoted to preserving the right of free speech on the Internet.
Privacy International https://www.privacyinternational.org/	Privacy International's mission is to defend the right to privacy across the world and to fight surveillance and other intrusions into private life by governments and corporations.
Internet Privacy Coalition (IPC) http://www.crypto.org/	The mission of the IPC is to promote privacy and security on the Internet through widespread public availability of strong encryption and the relaxation of export controls on cryptography.
Liberty http://www.liberty-human-rights.org.uk/	Liberty is a UK organization also known as the National Council for Civil Liberties. Founded in 1934, Liberty has no political affiliation and campaigns for the protection of fundamental rights and freedoms in the UK.
Online Privacy Alliance (OPA) http://www.privacyalliance.org/	OPA is a consortium of 21 organizations (including Microsoft, IBM and Sun) and nine associations working to support privacy in a free-market, self-regulated manner. The OPA has published its own set of privacy principles, which are somewhat streamlined in comparison to most other frameworks. Also, the OPA has developed a set of principles for self-regulation and certification of privacy conformance.

Privacy Rights Clearinghouse (PRC)
www.privacyrights.org
	Per the PRC Mission and Goals, the PRC is a "nonprofit consumer organization with a two-part mission: consumer information and consumer advocacy. Established in 1992, the PRC is based in San Diego, California, and is primarily grant-supported and serves individuals nationwide."[31]
	    The PRC's goals include: raising consumer awareness; empowering consumers to take action; responding to specific privacy-related complaints; documenting the nature of consumers' complaints and questions; and advocating for consumers' privacy rights in local, state, and federal public policy.[32]
	    The PRC also offers consumer services that include: consumer hotline, fact sheets, web site for data retrieval, referral services for journalists and policy makers, and speakers.

PrivacyExchange www.privacyexchange.org/	"PrivacyExchange is an online global resource for consumer privacy and data protection. It contains a library of privacy laws, practices, publications, websites and other resources concerning consumer privacy and data protection developments worldwide."[33]
TRUSTe https://www.truste.org	TRUSTe is an independent, corporate-sponsored, nonprofit privacy initiative dedicated to building users' trust and confidence on the Internet and accelerating growth of the Internet industry. They have developed a third-party oversight "seal" program with the aim of alleviating users' concerns about online privacy.

2.1.6 Element 6: Industry Frameworks

Industry frameworks may be internationally or nationally based to support various principles and provide privacy frameworks within different taxonomies (the conception, naming and classification of data groups). They are typically not covered in laws, regulations, or standards. For example:

- Canadian Standards Association (CSA) Privacy Code
- International Organization for Standardization (ISO) released ISO 17799/ British Standards BS7799
- International Security, Trust, and Privacy Alliance (ISTPA)
- Organisation for Economic Co-operation and Development (OECD)
- Payment Card Industry (PCI) Data Security Standard (PCI DSS) PCI Security Standards Council for PCI, PTS, PA-DAA
- Specific privacy program frameworks:
  - APEC Privacy Framework: A framework to enable regional data transfers to benefit consumers, businesses and governments.
  - Privacy by Design solutions: Built by organizations to ensure consumers' privacy protections at every stage in developing their products. These include reasonable security for consumer data, limited collection and retention of such data, and reasonable procedures to promote data accuracy.
  - U.S. government, FTC: Recommendations for Business and Policy Makers.
  - AICPA/CICA Generally Accepted Privacy Principles (GAPP).

Some of these are defined below.

Table 2.9: Industry Frameworks

AICPA and CICA Privacy Framework	The American Institute of Certified Public Accountants (AICPA) and the Canadian Institute of Chartered Accountants (CICA) have responded to requests for privacy certification by creating a program called WebTrust. Through this program, accountants can become certified to conduct privacy evaluations, such as Canada's Privacy Impact Assessment (PIA). Given the differences in standards across nations, territories and states, the AICPA and the CICA jointly developed a privacy framework based on a holistic approach to multinational privacy laws.
ISO 17799/BS7799	The International Organization for Standardization (ISO) released ISO 17799 in December 2000. It is a standard for information security practices and is a derivative of the British Standards BS7799. The latest versions of the two are functionally equivalent. The standard is required practice for all government departments in the UK; several other countries have adopted the standard as well (including Australia, Brazil, Japan, Netherlands, and Sweden). In relation to privacy, the standard contains several controls for ensuring data quality and the security of personal information. However, the standard focuses on securing sensitive information rather than dealing with sensitive personal information.
ISTPA Privacy Framework	The International Security, Trust, and Privacy Alliance (ISTPA) is an industry organization focused on creating actionable frameworks for businesses implementing data protection policies. The ISTPA published its Privacy Framework 1.1 in October, 2002. More than just a framework for public policy, the ISTPA framework provides sufficient technical detail to benefit IT architects, software developers and privacy consultants.
OECD Privacy Guidelines (OECD)	The Organisation for Economic Co-operation and Development is a group focused on reducing friction in international business relationships. The OECD membership is made up of representatives from 30 countries, including most of Europe, the U.S. and Australia. The group developed guidelines for member states to follow as they draft privacy legislation; the guidelines are often used today as a standard tool for assessing adherence to privacy rights.
CSA Privacy Code (CSA)	The Canadian Standards Association (CSA) Privacy Code (originally called the Model Code for the Protection of Personal Information) became a national standard in 1996 and formed the basis for Canada's PIPEDA legislation. The code itself is based on the OECD guidelines, to which Canada was a signatory. In contrast to the seven principles in the OECD guidelines, however, Canada's privacy code includes ten principles (the same principles as in PIPEDA).

2.1.7 Element 7: Privacy-Enhancing Technologies

Privacy-Enhancing Technologies (PETs) could be considered a technical control, but instead they should be thought of as an extension to technical controls for improving the quality of information and privacy choice control mechanisms available. As an example, the U.S. government has required agencies to offer machine-readable privacy policies using the Platform for Privacy Preferences (P3P) system.

These PETs reside above the general technical controls on automated systems; thus they rely on the protections from those to further strengthen and meet certain specifications, requirements or mandates. As with technical controls, the privacy professional should use a subject matter expert to assist with this highly technical topic. Below is an example of some of the PETs languages and protocols used today. The privacy professional should not try to interpret this data. Instead, privacy professionals should gather and track the relevant data from the organization to document the facts for user later in privacy management.

Table 2.10: Privacy Languages and Protocols

Language/Protocol	Description
Platform for Privacy Preferences (P3P)	P3P is a machine-readable language that helps to express a website's data management practices in an automated fashion.
Enterprise Privacy Authorization Language (EPAL) relies on authorization language	A formal language for writing enterprise privacy policies to govern data handling practices in IT systems according to fine-grained positive and negative authorization rights.
Extensible Access Control Markup Language (XACML) 1.0	Request-response-style language for determining access privileges, as well as a routine for discovering policy.
Liberty Alliance and SAML	The Liberty Alliance Project is an industry consortium that develops specifications for federated identity management, single sign on (SSO), account linking and global logout in online e-business environments.

2.1.8 Element 8: Privacy Innovation

Privacy innovation concerns are those not covered under the other privacy elements. These are items such as technology, standards and policy not yet categorized or owned by one of the other elements. As an example, data masking and runtime aliasing are considered privacy innovations that should be documented and tracked through the privacy functions.

The requirements in this element are fulfilled by reviewing all previous elements in researching any cutting-edge or innovative trends that are not defined or included in many privacy practices today. Many times innovations will come from the privacy organization or frameworks; thus this task is not easy, as it requires much research and effort.

Once the business case is defined based on the eight elements, it is time to move on to the next phase: to assemble the team.

2.1.9 Element 9: Education and Awareness

Education and awareness as a basic rule reinforce the organization privacy policy and practices. Education allows for communication and socialization of the privacy policy and supporting processes, to include formal and informal methods that may be recorded in the employee records. It is critical to the successful delivery of the privacy message and sets the stage for reception and acceptance throughout the organization. Education methods include: classroom training; online learning through streaming, videos and websites; poster campaigns; booklets; workshops, etc. The education strategy and budget typically determine the best or approved methods for education within the organization. The privacy professional should first understand those to ensure they align and meet those standards before offering any solutions.

> *Have a regular coffee and catch-up on one privacy topic via a 15-minute web conference or a face-to-face meeting.*

An organization's privacy awareness program reinforces the privacy message through reminders, continued advertisement, and other methods. Reinforcement of these facts ensures greater privacy awareness that can effectively reduce the risk of privacy data breach or accidental disclosure. Awareness methods include posters, flyers and trinkets, such as pencils, pens, notepads, etc.

Some mistakes typically associated with education and awareness include:

1. Equating education to awareness

2. Using only one communication channel

3. Lack of effectiveness measurements

4. Eliminating either education or awareness due to budget concerns

> *Awareness-raising is one of the key aspects of the privacy framework and should be prioritized for all organizations. This can come in different shapes and forms and in waves, none of which require huge amounts of resources and budgets. If people are not aware of what they are processing, they are also unaware of the consequences and liabilities that come with that ignorance.*

2.1.10 Element 10: Program Assurance, Including Audits, or the Governance Structure

The governance structure should mandate operational safeguards that include auditing. Auditing provides a method to prove accountability and compliance to the organization's objectives, as well as to laws and regulations. Auditors focus on the identification of threats to the organization's data through inspection, research and benchmarking. Results from those efforts can be ranked according to the likelihood of occurrence and impact. Assigning values to threats will highlight the strongest and weakest controls, policies and procedures, thus allowing the organization to focus on identifying and mitigating threats to the organization. Audit methods may include, but are not limited to:

- **Audits.** An independent assessment of whether your data protection policies and procedures are adequate and whether they are being followed in practice.

- **Privacy Assessments.** Several legal and regulatory oversight agencies require or recommend privacy assessments to include Privacy Impact Assessments (PIAs). As an example, by U.S. federal law, the E-Government Act of 2002 (Public Law 107–347) requires federal agencies to conduct Privacy Impact Assessments (PIAs) for electronic IT systems that collect, maintain or disseminate PII and to make these assessments publicly available.[34] There are also privacy impact frameworks in Australia, Canada, Hong Kong, Ireland, New Zealand and the UK. These frameworks were examined in a report prepared for the European Commission, which is available at http://www.piafproject.eu/ref/PIAF_D1_21_Sept_2011.pdf.

- **Privacy and Audit Management.** This provides key aspects of privacy management, to include: staff management process; audit planning; collecting, handling and data analysis for storage, use and transmission. Best practices recommend use of a standardized audit framework, such as Control Objectives for Information and Related Technology (CobiT). CobiT provides a reference model for good controls that allows for business needs to be aligned under one "umbrella" of control.[35]

For organizations that are already under the obligation to annually recertify adherence to the EU-U.S./Swiss-U.S. Safe Harbor frameworks, it is good practice to also use that as an exercise to assess the organization's current privacy practices.

2.2 Gap Analysis

Performing a gap analysis will determine the capability of current privacy management to support each of the business and technical requirements uncovered in the previous phase, if any exist. The gap analysis should be conducted any time you wish to understand the organizational change to the business case or mission statement. This phase requires reviewing the capabilities of current systems, management tools, hardware, operating systems, administrator expertise, system locations, outsourced services and physical infrastructure. While reviewing those capabilities or others, the goal is to determine the progress made towards organizational privacy requirements.

> *Consider performing the gap analysis as an assess-and-coach session for each area/region of the organization's business. The privacy expert can assess the current privacy processes and procedures as well as provide coaching in enhancements and improvements. These sessions can be documented along with the improvements and then used to monitor progress in the future.*

During this review, privacy professionals should use their knowledge of technologies and current industry trends and directions to evaluate privacy management objectives of the organization to consider:

- Alignment with business strategies, objectives and goals
- The effectiveness of technical design and use of controls
- Project, program and organization risk
- Cost
- Measurement of the technical and management environment

If gaps are found, they should be documented to include all facts that support the claim, so they can be used to provide corrective measures, mitigations or updates as necessary. Gaps should not be thought of as bad or incorrect but instead as a path forward to correct or update those findings. The governance structure of the organization should be contacted to inform them of the findings and actions to allow them stakeholder input, refinement and direction when necessary. Some gaps may be small and not important enough to report, while others may be so severe the organization may have to institute change as quickly as possible.

> *Any deficiencies found during a gap analysis could be addressed in a step-by-step approach by making priorities, which will depend on the type of business the organization is in. In addition, understanding how the organization does compared to its peers and competitors through benchmarking very often serves as a good tool when choosing which gaps to address first, as good data protection practices are seen more and more as a competitive advantage.*

2.3 Review Process and Monitoring

Establishing a review process or monitoring for the framework details allows for review of changes to the privacy framework and impacts to the organization. This can be done during the business and system life cycle changes or on a schedule, such as biannually or yearly or whatever meets the organizational need. The privacy team should establish a regular schedule of follow-up meetings to review the framework, determine areas that must be revisited, perform gap analysis and implement any required changes.[36]

2.4 Communicate the Framework to Internal and External Stakeholders

Your stakeholders, internal and external, will have been defined during the business case development phase of the framework, and they will be the target audience for framework communication and documentation. The stakeholders and framework development should be created early in the system development life cycle and updated on a continuous basis as a living breathing document that aligns to changes in the organization. Communication of the framework will follow best practices for formal and informal methods of communication that include:

- **Meetings.** Vary depending on organization size.
- **Conference Calls.** This is a less expensive method to bring many people together using technology, rather than travel to one site. These can also be recorded for replay later on.
- **Formal Education and Awareness.** Utilizes a classroom environment to deliver official training that may be recorded and documented.
    - **E-Learning.** Content is delivered via Internet-type services that electronically support learning and teaching through computer-based training (CBT), Internet-based training (IBT) or web-based training (WBT).
    - **Newsletters/E-mail/Posters.** This one method of education and awareness used for many years. Delivery methods include e-mail, website, physical displays, as well as many others through technology, print and verbal delivery.
    - **Video Teleconferencing.** Delivery of content via computer video similar to YouTube™ with videos that can be recorded live and replayed.
    - **Web Pages.** Online web pages provide an electronic media to reflect communication of data, knowledge bases, frequently asked questions, etc.
    - **Voice-mail Broadcast.** Provides an automated means to deliver a message (broadcast) to all the employees without having to contact each one separately.

Communication should be constant at all levels of the organization and stakeholders to ensure they understand the framework and how it impacts and improves the organization.

3. Summary

In summary, as part of privacy program governance, the privacy policy framework identifies the tasks involved in developing organizational privacy policies, standards and/or guidelines. This is the first step necessary for the privacy professional to create an individually tailored framework.

Table 2.11 is a template provided to assist with the development of the privacy policy framework as outlined in this chapter.

Table 2.11: Privacy Policy Framework Template

Task	Description
A. The Business Case 1. Organizational privacy office guidance 2. Define privacy 3. Laws and regulations 4. Technical security controls 5. External privacy organizations 6. Industry frameworks 7. Privacy information technology languages and protocols 8. Information technology cutting Innovation 9. Education and awareness 10. Program assurance	
B. Gap Analysis	
C. Review Process and Monitoring	

With the abundance of data privacy concerns, ever-changing laws and regulations, the increase in social networking and use of personal data, and continued advancements in the use of technology in everyday life, the privacy professional's tasks will continue to evolve, and vigilance is required. As privacy, privacy management, privacy governance, and all things privacy become more and more complex, the privacy professional needs flexible and reusable best practices to adapt to changes in technology and business and create solid privacy programs. These programs need to evolve as the culture, technology and laws change; otherwise gaps will form between privacy management and the external expectations of the privacy world.

Frameworks in the form of reusable structures, checklists, templates, processes and procedures prompt and remind the privacy professional of the details necessary to determine all privacy-relevant decisions in the organization. Having this framework and blueprint provides clear guidance on protecting data privacy to align with the expectations, requirements and laws, as well as the public demands for handling personal information safely and respectfully. The privacy program framework found in this chapter provides fundamental guidance on the many factors all organizations should consider for privacy program management, regardless of geographical location, local laws or regulations. The framework reveals a vast array of topics and tasks that each organization must consider within a system life cycle approach to data privacy management and solutions.

The business benefits of an effective, reusable framework are significant and include lower risk solutions; reducing the risk of data loss; sustaining market value and reputation; supporting business commitment and objectives to stakeholders, customers, partners and vendors; and compliance to laws, regulations and industry standards. This privacy program framework thereby provides an implementation roadmap to guide and prompt the privacy professional, privacy leader or privacy office about the details necessary to determine privacy-relevant decisions for the organization to document those, identify gaps, and mitigate them.

There is no one-size-fits-all privacy standard. This privacy program framework provides the necessary information and design patterns to build and manage an effective privacy program. It allows an adaptable and flexible approach to assist in making strategic business decisions in the selection of methods, strategies and technologies for the protection and privacy concerns of data usage today. This provides the architectural guidance and framework to associate current privacy standards to that of data privacy protection within business objectives and goals. This reusable framework thereby identifies privacy-related tasks so risk can be mitigated and the organization can be protected. Implementing the framework is only the first cornerstone to protecting privacy in the organization but will provide the foundation for effective privacy management.

Endnotes

1 www.apec.org/Groups/Committee-on-Trade-and-Investment/~/media/Files/Groups/ECSG/05_ecsg_privacyframewk.ashx.

2 *Id.*

3 Department of Justice of Canada, *Personal Information Protection and Electronic Documents Act*, (S.C. 2000, C.5) laws-lois.justice.gc.ca/eng/acts/P-8.6/index.html.

4 Australian Government, Office of the Australian Information Commissioner, *Information Privacy Principles*, www.privacy.gov.au/law/act/ipp.

5 Organisation for Economic Co-operation and Development. *OECD Guidelines Governing the Protection of Privacy and Transborder Flows of Personal Data*, Sept. 23, 1980. An important distinction between the OECD and the COE is the involvement and support of the United States government. For more information, see www.oecd.org/document/18/0,3343, en_2649_34255_1815186_1_1_1_1,00.html.

6 www.whitehouse.gov/sites/default/files/privacy-final.pdf.

7 Federal Trade Commission, *Protecting Consumer Privacy in an Era of Rapid Change: Recommendations for Businesses and Policymakers* (2012), http://ftc.gov/os/2012/03/120326privacyreport.pdf.

8 Dan Blum. *How to Develop an Identity Management Architecture Using Burton Group's Reference Architecture*, The Burton Group. January 2006. PDF.

9 CDT Mission and Principles, www.cdt.org/mission (last modified 2012).

10 *Id.*

11 William B. Baker and Anthony Matyjaszewski, *The changing meaning of "personal data,"* September 30, 2010, www.privacyassociation.org/resource_center/the_changing_meaning_of_personal_data.

12 *Id.*

13 Organisation for Economic Co-operation and Development, *OECD Guidelines on the Protection of Privacy and Transborder Flows of Personal Data*, www.oecd.org/internet/interneteconomy/oecdguidelinesontheprotectionofprivacyandtransborderflowsofpersonaldata.htm#guidelines.

14 Blum. *How to Develop an Identity Management Architecture* at 24.

15 This strategy often resembles a "seed" model, whereby the beginnings are small but eventually grow in complexity and completeness (Google Wikipedia).

16 The International Association of Privacy Professionals, Data Protection Authorities, www.privacyassociation.org/resource_center/data_protection_authorities.

17 Herath, *Building a Privacy Program*, 30.

18 *Id.* at 32.

19 42 U.S.C. § 1320d-5, www.law.cornell.edu/uscode/html/uscode42/usc_sec_42_00001320---d005-.html.

20 www.justice.gov/opcl/1974crimpen.htm.

21 Tom Brewster, *ICO Sony Data Breach Decision Coming in Six Weeks*, March 28, 2012, http://www.techweekeurope.co.uk/news/ico-sony-data-breach-decision-coming-in-six-weeks-69888.

22 The Charter of Fundamental Rights of the European Union: Data Protection in the European Union: the role of National Data Protection Authorities. 2010. PDF.

23 Privacy Commissioner for Personal Data (PCPD), Hong Kong. URL: http://www.pcpd.org.hk/.

24 Nicole V. Crain and W. Mark Crain, "The Regulation Tax Keeps Growing," *The Wall Street Journal,* September 27, 2010. http://online.wsj.com/article/SB10001424052748703860104575508122499 819564.html.

25 Office of Management and Budget, Office of Information and Regulatory Affairs, *2009 Report to Congress on the Benefits and Costs of Federal Regulations and Unfunded Mandates on State, Local, and Tribal Entities,* p. 3, 2009. www.whitehouse.gov/sites/default/files/omb/assets/legislative_ reports/2009_final_BC_Report_01272010.pdf.

26 Statenet, "Protecting Your Bottom Line through Monitoring Government Regulation 2," http:// beepdf.com/doc/127381/protecting_your_bottom_line_through_monitoring_government_ regulation.html (Last modified 2011).

27 IAPP, "Privacy Professionals Role, Function and Salary Survey," 27 www.privacyassociation.org/ media/pdf/knowledge_center/IAPP_Salary_Survey_2012.pdf.

28 ISO 27001 standards as found at the ISO 27001 Directory at URL: http://www.27000.org/iso-27001.htm. HTML.

29 ISO 27002 standards as found at the ISO 27002 Directory at URL: http://www.27000.org/iso-27002.htm. HTML.

30 "About the ACLU," www.aclu.org/about-aclu-0.

31 "Privacy Rights Clearing House Mission and Goals," www.privacyrights.org/about_us.htm#goals.

32 *Id.*

33 "Privacy Exchange Welcome," www.privacyexchange.org/.

34 www.gpo.gov/fdsys/pkg/PLAW-107publ347/pdf/PLAW-107publ347.pdf.

35 IT Governance Institute, "CobiT 4.1 Excerpt: Executive Summary Framework," p. 7, www.isaca. org/Knowledge-Center/cobit/Documents/COBIT4.pdf.

36 Blum. *How to Develop an Identity Management Architecture* at 06.

CHAPTER THREE

Performance Measurement

This chapter will assist the privacy professional with best practices in generic terms to identify, define, select, collect and analyze metrics specific to privacy.

With profound advances in both the technology and data exchange methods of the last few years and of the legal obligations imposed, each organization must ensure proper data protections are in place within businesses and between employees, consumers and customers. Tracking and benchmarking data protection indicators through performance measurement is important to ensure they are current and provide adequate protection and value to the organization.

> *[A]s privacy matures, as privacy is seen for its risk management capabilities, as privacy gets more engrained in business operations, better metrics relating to privacy are needed.*
>
> —*Ian Glazer, Gartner, April 2010*[1]

Products, services and systems that cannot provide value or protect data must change; otherwise, loss of information through catastrophic data loss (breach), noncompliance with regulatory requirements or data misuse could threaten a business through loss of consumer and investor confidence and financial loss and reflect very poorly on the organization in the commercial, social and public media.

Key Definitions
- *Performance Measurement. The process of formulating or selecting metrics to evaluate implementation, efficiency or effectiveness; gathering data and producing quantifiable output that describes performance*
- *Metrics. Tools that facilitate decision making and accountability through collection, analysis, and reporting of data. They must be measurable, meaningful, clearly defined (with boundaries), indicate progress, and answer a specific question to be valuable and practical.*

Organizations need a coherent method to inform leaders, managers, employees and all stakeholders how well the business is performing by using a fair and equitable measurement system that is easy to understand and reflects relevant indicators. Known as *performance measurement with metrics selection*, this process provides measurement methods by providing the means to evaluate business rhythms, technical systems and associated costs to the strategic business objectives and performance of the organization. Metrics performance provides quantifiable output that is *measurable, meaningful, answers specific questions and is clearly defined.* As a basic rule, metrics must add value and provide data tracking to improve business objectives and goals. Objectives are typically broad-based (e.g., privacy notices), while goals are specific and measurable (e.g., provide privacy notices to 100 percent of the customer base; number of privacy notices).

Metrics are gathered for a number of purposes and provide data that facilitate decision making and improve performance through the monitoring of regulatory compliance, as well as increased accountability through the collection, analysis and reporting of relevant information (e.g. business, technical, budgetary, etc.). The result provides the measurements necessary to make informed decisions that improve on the efficiency and effectiveness of business systems, processes, technology solutions and use of resources.

> **Metrics performance** *must be measurable, meaningful, clearly defined (with boundaries), indicate progress and answer a specific question to be valuable and practical.*

Specific to the privacy professional, metrics increases the understanding of how the organization provides data privacy protections that meet laws, regulations, policy, best practices, stakeholder and consumer concerns. Privacy metrics assist leaders with the measurement, interrogation and data analysis of current business rhythms to meet privacy goals and objectives. Major drivers impacting the increased need for privacy metrics include:

- A means of providing meaningful information on your privacy regime to key stakeholders
- Generational change in the use of technology
- Rapid advancements to technology (i.e., mobile solutions, iPad, iPhone, etc.)
- Rapid societal change in the use of advanced technology (i.e., Facebook, Twitter, etc.)
- Catastrophes, such as data loss events, that drive tighter regulations, laws and standards

- Current security and privacy solutions that are not designed to deal with the fast pace of emerging technologies or requirements (i.e., cloud computing)
- Privacy regulations becoming more stringent while privacy expectations rise
- Professionals embrace security and privacy as part of their job

Metrics provide a common language between business, operational and technical managers to discuss the relevant information (e.g., good, bad or indifferent) related to assessing progress. They also allow information to be exchanged in the same language from senior leadership through project management to the technical management of any system without restrictions or complex jargon. Metrics must be described in and used with clear language and easy-to-understand terms; otherwise they may not represent similar value throughout an organization. For example, generic privacy metrics should be developed to enable analyses of the following processes:

- Collection (notice)
- Responses to data subject inquiries
- Use
- Retention
- Disclosure to third parties
- Incidents (breaches, complaints, inquiries)
- Employee training
- Privacy Impact Assessments (PIAs)
- Privacy risk indicators
- Percent of organization functions represented by governance mechanisms

Use of that data for analysis and reporting includes:

- Trending
- Privacy program return on investment (ROI)
- Business resiliency metrics
- Privacy program maturity level
- Resource utilization

The selection of the proper metrics is difficult, and special consideration must be used during the process for selection, use and updates. More metrics do not necessarily translate into more value. The old adage "You can never have enough" is incorrect regarding using metrics; data collection, storage and analysis are expensive business functions and are thus more costly when collecting unnecessary data or an extreme number of metrics that provide no value.

1. The Metric Life Cycle

Once a metric is selected, it is similar to any other business rhythm, technical solution or process. It must be maintained and managed throughout a life cycle to address changes with technology, business decisions, business objectives and the life of those systems. Without proper care and feeding, a metric could become stale and provide no further value. As illustrated in the program framework and privacy operational life cycle, metrics should be reviewed and data points added, changed or removed based on the ever-changing needs of the organization and stakeholders and the impacts of external functions, such as laws and regulations. The privacy professional should consider using that framework and/or life cycle as a standard practice to assist with metrics management and ensure sustainability.

> **Metric life cycle.** *The processes and methods to sustain a metric to match the ever-changing needs of an organization.*

Figure 3.1: Five-Step Metric Life Cycle

With a clear understanding and definition of metrics, why we need metrics, and the value they provide, we must now review the steps necessary to identify, define, select, collect and analyze the metric data. As shown in the figure above, the Five-Step Metric Life Cycle includes these key concepts:

- **Identification** of the intended audience: *who* will use the data?
- **Definition** of data sources: *who* is the data owner and *how* is that data accessed?
- **Selection** of privacy metrics: *what* metrics to use based on the audience, reporting resources and final selection of the best metric?
- **Collection** and **refinement** of systems/application collection points: *where* will the data come from to finalize the metric collection report? *When* will the data be collected? *Why* is that data important?
- **Analyze** the data/metrics to provide value to the organization and provide a feedback quality mechanism.

Metrics are gathered for a number of purposes and uses, including the program managers' use and capture of metrics relating to schedule, staffing or budget, and the stakeholders' tracking of budget to understand the rate of expenditure. As Blakely states, "The purpose of a metric and reporting system is to develop and help an organization define and measure progress towards a goal [and objective]."[2] Metrics may also help the privacy organization identify risks. A quote from Steve McConnell, author of numerous books on metrics, sums it up nicely: "There are no secrets on a successful project. Both good and bad news must be able to move up and down the project hierarchy without restriction. Metrics help IT and business speak the same language. Metrics provide each with valuable information that allows them to assess their progress toward a common goal."[3]

1.1 Step 1: Identify the Intended Audience for Metrics

The first step in selecting the correct metrics for any organization starts by identifying the intended metric audience—the relevant stakeholders who use this data to view, discuss and possibly make organizational strategic decisions based on this data. There is no limitation on this audience—the stakeholders could be internal or external to the organization, based on the data and reporting requirements. For example, one metric may be used for the internal board of directors, while another supports external auditors.

> ***Metric audience.*** *Primary, secondary and tertiary stakeholders who obtain value from a metric.*

The **primary audience** may include:
- Legal and privacy officers
- Senior leadership; chief information officer (CIO)
- Chief security officer (CSO)
- Program managers (PM)
- Information system owner (ISO)
- Information security officer (ISO)
- Others considered users and managers

The **secondary audience** includes those who may not have privacy as a primary task, such as:
- Chief financial officer (CFO)
- Training organizations
- Human resources (HR)
- Inspectors general (IG)
- HIPAA security officials

Tertiary audiences may be considered, based on the organization's specific or unique requirements, such as:
- External watch dog groups
- Sponsors
- Stockholders

The difference between these audiences is based on the level of interest, influence and responsibility to privacy within the business objectives, laws and regulations, or ownership. For example, specific to *healthcare;* audiences may include a HIPAA privacy officer, medical interdisciplinary readiness team (MIRT), senior executive staff, covered entity workforce, self-assessment tool and risk analysis/management.

Stakeholders at all levels should be involved in the selection and management of any metric to ensure buy-in and a sense of ownership; otherwise metrics may be seen as negative, costly and adding no value. Consideration must include all layers of the organization to encourage the overall success and usefulness of any metric beyond the needs of the privacy professional, with group consensus for management and use.

1.2 Step 2: Define Reporting Resources

Since metrics continue to change as the business objectives and goals evolve, someone must be the champion and responsible owner of a metric to ensure it continues to meet the requirements and needs of the business, is relevant and provides value. A *metric owner* must be able to evangelize the purpose and intent of that metric to the organization. As a best practice, it is highly recommended a person with privacy knowledge, training and experience performs this role to limit possible errors within interpretation of privacy related laws, regulations and practices.

> *Metric owner. Process owner, champion, advocate and evangelist responsible for management of the metric throughout the metric life cycle.*

As Six Sigma teaches, an effective metric owner must:

1. **Know what is critical about the metric.** Why the output is important and understand how this metric fits into the business objectives.
2. **Monitor process performance with the metric.** Predictors of performance and monitoring data compiled by other metric owners, processes, or dependencies (operations, strategic, or tactical).
3. **Make sure the process documentation is up to date.** This ensures all audiences have a clear definition of the metric and how it should be used. Many times, organizations allow too much variance within a metric. The owners must champion and develop documentation of metrics using flowcharts, visual displays, graphics and other methods. They must also champion the metric in meetings, working groups and in other organization communications.
4. **Perform regular reviews.** Determine if the metric is still required, capable to meet goals, and provides value to the organization.
5. **Make sure that any improvements are incorporated and maintained in the process.**

6. **Advocate the metric to customers, partners, and others.**
7. **Maintain training, documentation, and materials.**

As a general practice, the metric owner may not perform the data collection tasks or perform the measurements of the metric. As an example, the tasks may be directed to the IT department, and the metric owner simply utilizes the information. The metric owner ensures the usefulness, business need and value of the metric to the organization. Data collection, a different topic, will be addressed in Section 1.4 of this chapter.

1.3 Step 3: Select Privacy Metrics

After selecting the audience and defining the reporting resources of the metric owner, it is time to select relevant privacy metrics. As the next step in the metric life cycle, selecting the correct privacy metric requires a full understanding of the business objectives and goals, along with a clear understanding of the primary business functions. Prior to selecting metrics, the reader should first understand the *attributes of an effective metric with metric taxonomy and how to limit improper metrics.* After understanding those concepts, the privacy professional can proceed with metric selection, as shown in this chapter.

1.3.1 Attributes of an Effective Metric

Knowing what metric to measure and report on is important in reflecting the business value of that metric. It will show the efficiency and effectiveness of the metric to the organization and how it is a value added to the organization. Since metrics are commonly mistrusted, misused, overused, and sometimes mismanaged, this section prepares the privacy professional to better understand those attributes that make a metric a successful representation of the efficiency and effectiveness of a process.

Effective metric. Clear and concise metric that defines and measures progress toward a business objective or goal without overburdening the reader.

Effective metrics define and measure progress toward business goals and objectives. Good metrics *should not overburden the reader,* thus the information should be concise and the metrics manageable in number. Producing large amounts of useless information is counterproductive, so selection should be made for key indicators with the greatest value and insight to the specific business case of the metric. The metric should also **be clear in the meaning of what is being measured, rigorously defined, credible and relevant, objective and quantifiable** and, finally, associated with the **baseline measurement** per the organization standard metric taxonomy.[4] Metric taxonomies assist with better understanding the characteristics associated with different metrics to ensure organizational coverage and utility of a metric. If a standard metric taxonomy does not exist, privacy professionals can generate their own using the best practices from the National Institute of Standards and Technology (NIST), NISTIR 7564, "Directions in Security Metrics Research."[5]

Without going into great detail on metric taxonomies, they provide the following categories:

- **Objective/Subjective.** Objective metrics are more desirable than subjective metrics.

- **Quantitative/Qualitative.** Qualitative measurements typically map to best practices, while quantitative measurements use data recorded within a numerical-mathematical fashion. Per recent industry surveys, chief information security officers (CISOs) seem to prefer qualitative measurements, as they better reflect the effectiveness of IT, IT security programs and IT privacy programs.

- **Information Technology Metrics/Quantitative Measurement.** Since IT generates many data points daily, this collection method easily exceeds millions to billions of bits of data. The privacy professional must not be confused or overwhelmed with technology but instead research and refine privacy metrics to harness this data.

- **Static/Dynamic.** Dynamic metrics evolve with time; static metrics do not.

- **Absolute/Relative.** Absolute metrics do not depend on other measures.

- **Direct/Indirect.** The distinction between direct and indirect metrics is based on the way a metric is measured. Size, for example, can be directly measured, whereas quality or complexity can only be measured indirectly by extrapolation from other measured factors.

Metric taxonomy list the metric characterizes that delineate boundaries between metric categories.

1.3.2 Limiting Improper Metrics

Metrics are sometimes used poorly or improperly or contain faulty assumptions. As a best practice, the privacy professional must be aware of these facts during metric management and life cycle to limit negative aspects and provide valid business value to the expenditure of organizational resources. The privacy professional must guard against:

- **Faulty Assumptions.** The conclusion is based on the occurrence of concurrent events without substantive evidence correlating the events.

- **Selective Use.** A specific subset of information is extrapolated from the larger data set, which leads to invalid/incorrect conclusions.

- **The Well-chosen Average.** Many times the mean (sum of the data/number of data points) is used for a metric, but it is sometimes more appropriate to use the median (middle value) or mode (most frequently occurring value) rather than the true mean/average.

- **Semi-attachment.** This results when an individual is unable to prove their point; semi-attachment may result, with the exclusion of elements of a measurement when conveying results.

- **Biased Sample.** This measurement completely excludes certain elements from the data population, thus providing only a partial set of data and leading to false assumptions.

- **Intentional Deceit.** An ethical issue, this occurs when data is knowingly and purposely omitted that may have a detrimental effect on the metric or metric owner.

- **Massaging the Numbers.** Although not as severe as intentional deceit, this category could also be unethical. It involves "massaging" the measurements to provide the appearance of success or other than actual results, leading the reviewer to believe the metric is more successful than it actually may be.

- **Overgeneralization.** This occurs when inferences are made concerning a general data population that leads to poor conclusions; for example, extrapolating limited experiences and evidence to broad generalizations.

Even with known maturity within the market place, the automation tools and other standards, there are still organizations with weak metrics. In recent interviews, CIOs acknowledged using weak metrics that could be improved. One CIO acknowledged that a group did not know how to measure itself, the organization or processes. The privacy metric owner must guard against general weaknesses identified above, as well as others yet to be determined. Simply knowing that metrics are not perfect and they need management are the first steps to proper life cycle management.

1.3.3 SMART Methodology

With a full understanding of the intended audience, reporting resource and attributes of an effective metric and how to limit improper metrics, the privacy professional is now ready to start selecting appropriate metrics.

Six Sigma is a data-driven quality methodology first developed by Motorola in the 1980s.[6] The SMART—specific/simple, manageable, actionable, relevant/results-oriented, and timely—method was developed as part of Six Sigma as a tool for defining goals. This framework can be applied successfully for determining the proper metric. SMART includes:

- Specific/simple. Clear definition and is actionable, relevant and trending

- Manageable. Objective, independently verified, and obtainable

- Actionable. Reveals potential problems that can be fixed and helps drive improvement

- Relevant/results-oriented. Ensures metrics are determined within context of your organization

- Timely. Trending allows tracking over time for comparisons

Metrics must be **sustainable and improve** the organization; thus these factors also apply:

- **Goal:** Clearly define (with boundaries) what the organization hopes to achieve
- **Objective:** Answer a specific question
- **Evidence of value:** Prove value add
- **Level of effectiveness:** Is data collection and reporting effective and efficient

Regardless of the characteristics, all data reporting must be standardized and agreed upon by all stakeholders. Adjustments should be made to ensure accurate, complete and valid reporting each and every time, without confusion, mixed results or errors. Not all data is useful for metrics; thus the privacy professional must verify and validate any data collection efforts. The primary focus must be to maximize usefulness of the metric rather than simple data collection. Benefits should outweigh the costs of investing resources to maintain and maximize the benefits of the metric collection. This will be further addressed in the metric selection process.

As a basic business practice in the selection of metrics, the privacy professional should select **three to five** key privacy metrics that focus on the key organizational objectives. They can then assist other functions with other metrics that may have privacy implications.

> **Total number of metrics.** *Select three to five metrics to start with; refine requirements for additional metrics later.*

1.3.4 Metric Template

A standard format will provide the detail required to guide measures for collection, analysis and reporting activities. The metrics template, provided in Table 3.1, is an example of such a format, based on the National Institute of Standards and Technology (NIST) "Performance Measurement Guide for Information Security," Special Publication (SP) 800-55, revision 1.[7] This template provides a suggested approach to metric development. Based on internal practices and procedures, organizations may tailor their own performance measurement templates by using a subset of these fields or adding more fields based on their environment and requirements.

Table 3.1: Sample Metrics Template

Field	Data
Metric Name/ ID	States the unique identifier that uses an organization-specific naming convention or can directly reference another source.
Goal	Statement of the organization goal. When possible, include both the enterprise-level goal and the specific information-security goal extracted from agency documentation, or identify an information security program goal that would contribute to the accomplishment of the selected strategic goal.

Measure	Statement of measurement. Use a numeric statement that begins with "percentage," "number," "frequency," "average" or a similar term. As an example, If applicable, list the NIST SP 800-53 security control(s) being measured. Security controls that provide supporting data should be stated in Implementation Evidence. If the measure is applicable to a specific FIPS 199 impact level (high, moderate or low), state this level within the measure.
Type	Statement of whether the measure is of implementation, effectiveness/efficiency or impact.
Formula	Calculation to be performed that results in a numeric expression of a measure. The information gathered through listing implementation evidence serves as an input into the formula for calculating the measure.
Target	Threshold for a satisfactory rating for the measure, such as a milestone completion or a statistical measure. Target can be expressed in percentages, time, dollars or other appropriate units of measure. Target may be tied to a required completion time frame. Select final and interim targets to enable tracking of progress toward stated goal.
Implementation Evidence	Implementation evidence is used to compute the measure, validate that the activity is performed and identify probable causes of unsatisfactory results for a specific measure. • For manual data collection, identify questions and data elements that would provide the data inputs necessary to calculate the measure's formula, qualify the measure for acceptance, and validate provided information. • For each question or query, state the security control number, if possible. (Example NIST SP 800-53 security control) • For automated data collection, identify data elements that would be required for the formula, qualify the measure for acceptance, and validate the information provided.
Frequency	Indication of how often the data is collected and analyzed and how often the data is reported. Select the frequency of data collection based on a rate of change in a particular security control that is being evaluated. Select the frequency of data reporting based on external reporting requirements and internal customer preferences.
Responsible Parties	Indicate the following key stakeholders: • Information Owner: Identify organizational component and individual who owns required pieces of information • Information Collector: Identify the organizational component and individual responsible for collecting the data. (Note: If possible, Information Collector should be a different individual or even a representative of a different organizational unit than the Information Owner, to avoid the possibility of conflict of interest and ensure separation of duties. Smaller organizations will need to determine whether it is feasible to separate these two responsibilities.) • Information Customer: Identify the organizational component and individual who will receive the data
Data Source	Location of the data to be used in calculating the measure. Include databases, tracking tools, organizations or specific roles within organizations that can provide required information.
Reporting Format	Indicates how the measure will be reported, such as a pie chart, line chart, bar graph or other format. State the type of format or provide a sample.

Table 3.2 provides an example of using the metric template defined in Table 3.1.

Table 3.2: Metric Template Example: Awareness and Training Measure[8]

Field	Data
Measure ID	Security Training Measure 1 (or a unique identifier to be filled out by the organization)
Goal	• *Strategic Goal:* Ensure a high-quality work force supported by modern and secure infrastructure and operational capabilities. • *Privacy Goal:* Ensure that organization personnel are adequately trained to carry out their assigned information security-related duties and responsibilities.
Measure	Percentage (%) of information system security personnel that have received security training (see NIST SP 800-53 Controls: AT-3: Security Training for definitions)
Measure Type	Implementation
Formula	(Number of personnel that have completed security training within the past year/total number of information system security personnel) *100
Target	This should be a high percentage defined by the organization
Implementation Evidence	Are training records maintained? How many of those with significant privacy responsibilities have received the required training?
Frequency	Collection Frequency: Organization-defined (example: quarterly) Reporting Frequency: Organization-defined (example: annually, monthly, weekly, etc)
Responsible Parties	• Information Owner: Organization-defined (example: Training Manager) • Information Collector: Organization-defined (example: Information System Security Officer [ISSO], Training Manager, Privacy Officer) • Information Customer: Chief Information Officer (CIO), Information System Security Officer (ISSO), Senior Agency Information Security Officer (SAISO) (e.g., Chief Information Security Officer [CISO])
Data Source	Training and awareness tracking records
Reporting Format	Pie chart illustrating the percentage of personnel that have received training versus those who have not received training. If performance is below target, pie chart illustrating causes of performance falling short of targets

1.3.5 Other Network and Enterprise Metric Examples

Beyond those privacy metrics explained in the previous paragraphs, Table 3.3 provides other examples, to include IT Enterprise management, other incidents, and security related metrics. This list is a shorten version of the metric table shown in the MITRE paper *Cyber Resiliency Metrics*, Version 1.0, Rev. 1.[9]

Table 3.3: Other Metric Examples

Metric Identifier	Summary	Comments
Recovered Data	*Quality of restored/recovered/reconstituted data*	Higher values are better. This metric assumes that (1) levels of data quality have been defined and (2) ways of evaluating data quality have been established.
Data Lost Percent	*Percentage of data irrevocably lost*	Lower values are better. This metric assumes a clear definition of what it means for data to be lost, e.g., data has been corrupted or deleted and cannot be reliably reconstructed from backups or other data stores.
Data Lost Records	*Number of records lost*	Lower values are better.
Training	*Percentage of information-system security and privacy personnel that have received training*	Higher values are better. This metric assumes that resilience-aware security training (i.e., training that includes responsibilities and processes for coordination as part of security management/administration and security operations) has been established. For an example of how to specify this metric, see NIST SP 800-55, Measure 4: Awareness and Training.
Average Incident Time	*Average length of time between cyber and privacy incidents*	Lower values are better. This common security metric assumes a consistent method for (1) defining what constitutes an incident and (2) identifying when an incident occurs. It also assumes a time period during which incidents are observed (e.g., average length of time during the first calendar quarter; average length of time from [specified date] to the present).
Incident Recovery Time	*Average length of time to recover from incidents*	Lower values are better. This common security metric assumes a consistent method for identifying (1) when an incident begins and (2) when incident recovery is complete. It also assumes a time period during which incidents (and recovery from incidents) are observed (e.g., average length of time during the first calendar quarter; average length of time from [specified date] to the present). For an example of how to specify this metric, see CIS, Mean-Time to Incident Recovery.

Systems Compliance	*Percentage of systems in compliance with organizationally mandated configuration guidance*	Higher values are better. This metric assumes that systems have been identified and configuration requirements have been specified. For an example of how to specify this metric, see CIS, Percentage of Configuration Compliance.
Number of Privacy Incidents	*Percentage of privacy incidents reported within required timeframe per applicable incident category*	Higher values are better. This metric assumes that (1) what constitutes an incident has been defined, (2) incident categories have been established, and (3) a required timeframe for incident reporting has been established. For an example of how to specify this metric, see NIST SP 800-55, Measure 10: Incident Response.
Average Time Between Incidents	*Average length of time between cyber and privacy incidents*	Lower values are better. This common security metric assumes a consistent method for (1) defining what constitutes an incident and (2) identifying when an incident occurs. It also assumes a time period during which incidents are observed (e.g., average length of time during the first calendar quarter; average length of time from [specified date] to the present).
Average Time To Recover	*Average length of time for the organization to recover from damage caused by a privacy incident*	Lower values are better. This metric assumes that (1) what constitutes an incident is defined, (2) the time when an incident starts can be determined and (3) the time when recovery is complete can be determined. It also assumes a time period during which incidents are observed (e.g., average length of time during the first calendar quarter; average length of time from [specified date] to the present).
Percent Plans Exist	*Percentage of critical incident types for which pre-planned responses exist*	Higher values are better. This metric assumes that a set of critical incident types have been defined.
Time Mission Impacted	*Length of time a mission is negatively affected after an attack*	Lower values are better. This metric assumes that (1) a definition of what it means for a mission to be negatively affected has been established, (2) when a mission has been negatively affected can be determined and (3) when a mission is no longer negatively affected can be determined.

1.4 Step 4: Collect Systems/Application Collection Points

Generic data collection procedures establish:

- **How data is collected.** Describe the origin, how obtained, unit of measure, tool use, documentation, how informed if data changes.

- **When the data is collected.** Indicate exactly when data is collected.

- **Who is responsible for collecting and recording the data.** Describe roles and responsibilities in writing and exact details to reduce confusion.

- **Where is the data stored.** Document data storage to include forms, documents, e-mail along with storage data to include database, tool, and others.

- **How to ensure data accuracy.** Document the consistency checks that verify the data is reasonable and accurate. Describe these procedures in detail.

Reporting resources can be found with the technical and business characteristics of an organization that include:

- **People** relates to the intended audience as well as those that supply information, including internal and external stakeholders. These could be considered the same group defined as the intended audience for metrics in Section 1.1; thus, there are **primary**, **secondary** and **tertiary** sources. Examples include **HR, legal, privacy office.**

- **Processes** are business characteristics that are nontechnical but easy obtainable, relevant (e.g., add value) and measure improvements (e.g., benchmarks to target values).

- **Technology** includes quantifiable, repeatable and comparable data values. Examples include automated systems, information systems, etc.

The Software Productivity Center documents the following actions as being required for successful data collection:[10]

- Decide which data collection procedures are applicable

- Create any forms that are required for the collection

- Assign responsibility for metrics collection and ensure that the responsibility is agreed upon and documented

- Update any design or project documentation templates to include sections for data that must be collected

- Update the metrics documentation to include details on metrics collection procedures for the metrics coordinator(s)

- Optional: update any development process documentation to include relevant data collection procedures. Indicate which tasks and activities are affected

1.5 Step 5: Analyze the Data

Once step 3, "select privacy metrics," and step 4, "collection points," are accomplished, the last step, step 5, "analyze the data," will be accomplished using the collected data to perform analysis and create the performance metric. This step sometimes takes the most time of all five steps due the large amount of data collected on automated IT systems; thus, the privacy professional should consider use of automated tools or automated methods to gather, sort and report that data.

Data analysis can be done using automated software applications that perform statistical and financial functions and can be found within sources that include:

- Open source
- Public domain
- Freeware
- Commercial software

If advanced tools are not required, the privacy professional can always utilize standard business-based computer tools that include Microsoft® Access or Excel, or other products found on the Internet or within the organization. Selection and use of any tool should always be based on organization requirements, budget or direction. Once selected, the privacy professional can perform data analysis for trending, return on investment, business resiliency and program maturity as discussed in Chapter 1.

1.5.1 Trending

Trending, or trend analysis, is one of the easiest statistical methods used for reporting data. Statistical methods are required to ensure that data are interpreted correctly and that apparent relationships are meaningful and significant, not simply chance occurrences.

Trending practices collect information and attempts to spot a pattern, or trend, in the information as viewed over a period of time. There are many different "statistical trending" methods, including:

- Simple data patterns
- Fitting a trend: least-squares
- Trends in random data
- Data as trend plus noise
- Noisy time series
- Goodness of fit (R-squared)

Although each of these are good examples of trending, for simplicity sake, without going into a formal statistics explanations (e.g., mean, standard deviation, variance, linear trend, sample, population, signal, and noise), the privacy professional should only be concerned with the most basic trending example—that of looking for "data patterns," as the following examples:

- **Time series.** Trends are viewed in an upwards or downward tendency. Examples include number of privacy breaches over time.

- **Cyclical component.** Weekly, monthly or yearly data describing any regular fluctuations. Example: It is useful to measure the number of privacy breaches in the month after you rollout your new data protection training, and then every three months to see if the number steadily increases as distance from training increases. The practical use of the metric, and therefore the trending, is to help you to work out appropriate training intervals.

- **Irregular component.** This is the most difficult to detect; irregular component, or noise, is what is left over when the other components of the series (time and cyclical) have been accounted for. Examples include the absence or indication of privacy breaches.

1.5.2 Privacy Program Return on Investment (ROI)

"ROI is an indicator used to measure the financial gain/loss (or "value") of a project in relation to its cost."[11] By calculating ROI, an organization can assess whether the expense/investment is justified by the resulting savings/revenue. The most basic form of ROI calculation is:

$$ROI = (Benefits - Costs)/Costs$$

That is, the financial benefit after an investment or improvement is made minus the cost of the investment or improvement, calculated as a percentage of those costs. ROI is typically related to "decreased production costs" and "increased profit and revenue," but those don't apply to the privacy professional, at least not in this section. Thus we will say privacy ROI defines metrics to measure the effectiveness of investments to protect investments in:

- **Physical assets.** This term relates to the protection of hardware, software and data against physical threats, to reduce or prevent disruptions to operations and services and loss of assets.

- **Personnel assets.** Measures to reduce the likelihood and severity of accidental and intentional alteration, destruction, misappropriation, misuse, misconfiguration, unauthorized distribution and unavailability of an organization's logical and physical assets, as the result of action or inaction by insiders and known outsiders, like business partners.

- **Information technology (IT) assets.** Inherent technical features that collectively protect the organizational infrastructure, achieving, and sustaining, confidentiality, integrity, availability and accountability.

- **Operational management assets.** Implements standard operational procedures that define the interaction between users, systems and system resources. This ensures a known secure system state at all times and prevents accidental or intentional theft, release, destruction, alteration, misuse or sabotage of system resources.[12]

The ROI metric may not seem that important to the privacy professional, but it will be a major indicator to stakeholders for measuring investment to privacy protection and possibly further investments. These are sometimes defined by the organization leadership but can come from any of the stakeholders or data owners.

Consideration should be given to ROI analysis as related to fixed or variable data. This analysis should be a best attempt to perform an economical value risk assessment to determine the probability of a loss and the probable economic consequences. The goal is to maximize the benefits of investments that generally do not generate revenue; rather, they prevent loss. This analysis thereby provides the quantitative measurement for costs and benefits, strengths and weaknesses of the organization's privacy controls. This data can be fixed or variable. Fixed data is always consistent, while variable data can be any inconsistent value that is positive, negative or zero.

The first step is to identify and characterize the ROI metric to address the specific risk that control or feature is supposed to mitigate. This first step will calculate the ROI of the feature, function or control as related to the reason for implementing or installing that solution.[13]

The second step is to define the value of an asset. Since this is often difficult, the privacy professional must consider the value of an asset or information to the organization. The privacy professional should also remember that the value of this information or asset also changes over time and be prepared to adjust the ROI metric as necessary. Peltier has identified several parameters to consider when determining the value of information assets, to include:[14]

- The cost of producing the information
- The value of the information on the open market
- The cost of reproducing the information if it is lost, damaged or destroyed
- The benefit of the information in meeting the organization's mission and goals
- Repercussions to the organization if the information is not readily available when needed
- Advantages to a competitor if they can use, change or destroy the information
- The cost to the organization if the information were subject to unauthorized release, destruction or alteration
- The loss of public confidence in the organization if the information is not handled correctly
- The loss of credibility and embarrassment to the organization if the security of the information is compromised

1.5.3 Business Resiliency Metrics

As IBM states, "Business resilience is the ability to rapidly adapt and respond to business disruptions and to maintain continuous business operations, be a more trusted partner, and enable growth. True business resilience starts with understanding exactly what your business needs in order to survive unexpected events and plan ahead for challenges that could come at any time. Whether an event is IT related, business related, or a natural disaster, there will always be challenges to overcome. Think of business resilience as your ticket to continued business service and operational continuity—proper planning, readiness, and the ability to respond quickly to any threat or opportunity."[15]

Focusing solely on disasters will lead your organization to be defensive, but using a proactive approach enables the organization to "respond to an unexpected event more quickly and more cost-effectively. In addition to disaster situations, a strong business resilience program can help your organization prepare for audits and demonstrate compliance with regulatory requirements."[16]

To the privacy professional, business resiliency is measured through metrics associated with data privacy, system outages and other factors as defined by the business case and organization objectives. If it exists, the organization's business continuity or disaster recovery office should be contacted to assist in the selection and use of data for this metric type, as they are the experts in this data type and organizational objectives.

1.5.4 Resource Utilization

The privacy professional or organization should include in the privacy budget the costs to generate metrics. An example is provided by the International Association of Privacy Professionals' *2012 Privacy Professionals Role, Function and Salary Survey* data shown in the Figure 3.2. In 2012, the results of that survey found the most time-consuming task identified was of a strategic nature, that of advising the organization on privacy issues. Metric generation is listed under "monitoring and measuring privacy compliance" with the result of nine percent of the privacy office spent on metrics.

Figure 3.2: Resource Utilization

Time allocation	2011	2012	Change
STRATEGIC	32%	31%	-1%
Developing privacy strategy	8%	8%	0%
Analyzing privacy regulations	9%	8%	0%
Advising and consulting to the organization on privacy	15%	14%	0%
PROCESS	33%	32%	-1%
Developing and performing privacy training and communications	8%	8%	0%
Monitoring and measuring privacy compliance and enforcement	9%	9%	-1%
Responding to data incidents	8%	8%	0%
Reporting to management and privacy stakeholders	8%	7%	-1%
FOUNDATIONAL	23%	23%	0%
Performing privacy risk assessments and data inventories	8%	8%	0%
Developing and implementing privacy policies and guidance	10%	10%	0%
Administration of privacy personnel and budget	5%	4%	0%
ACTIVITIES NOT RELATED TO PRIVACY	14%	14%	0%

2. Summary

Metrics are used in this task to measure projects, track trends and reflect progress of many activities. Knoernschild says it best when he states, "You can't improve what you don't measure ... metrics serve as key performance indicators that can be used to set and attain [business] goals [and objectives]."[17] As described in this document, metrics need to be defined and agreed upon when retrofitting or at the start of any project, thus during the initial proposal phase and throughout the system life cycle. This provides the baseline measurement from the very beginning of the project, not after the project is approved and launched, through final implementation and use. Since program managers often change roles, providing the metric from the start allows any new management to understand the definition and intent of the metric as related to the core concepts of the project, thus achieving transparency from start to end. "Done correctly, metric development can provide key measures of IT [and privacy] efficiency, effectiveness, and value [to the organization]."[18]

This section provides both generic and specific metric details as applied to IT, IT security and privacy practices. Metric authors should consider the data presented in this section and consider the following objectives and goals upon choosing metrics:

- Must measure effectiveness and efficiency
- Must measure and improve business value of IT
- Increase project transparency and improve communication of IT relevant material within business context
- Ensure measurement is accurate, relevant and honest without intentional or unintentional effort
- Perform subjective evaluation of metrics throughout the metric life cycle
- Reassess on a scheduled basis to ensure they do not become stale or dated[19]
- Consider using qualitative and quantitative measurements with goals on metric maturity
- Consider laws and regulations for metric development, tracking and sharing with federal, state and local agencies
- Consider privacy as a shared security responsibility to ensure full coverage of all threats to the organization

Metrics must provide business value to the organization. As technology continues to advance at unprecedented rates and society finds new and different ways of using technology for data exchange and sharing, organizations, regardless of their location or industry, can no longer afford to ignore the issues and demands of data privacy and privacy practices. As Neuenschwander states, "Government regulations, consumer backlash, and security risks demand that information technology (IT) organizations place tighter controls on the personal information [PII] under their custodial control, including information on employees, partners, and customers."[20] Performance measurement provide the metrics to measure the daily business rhythms and provide the means to measure and grade how well an organization accomplishes the security and privacy tasks related to compliance issues, business value through ROI, meeting organizational objectives and goals and protecting all IT and non-IT resources as a foundational element of the organization. Tracking these benchmarks through metrics reflects that an organization is providing due diligence within adequate data protection and the identification of any weaknesses to reduce risk to the organization.

Privacy management in a wired world has become a complicated challenge for making informed choices and decisions on applying privacy-enhancing technology, process improvements and performance measurements. The privacy professional must be prepared for these challenges and to both adapt to and help drive innovation in the methods and best practices that track data privacy. Privacy professionals play an important role in teaching privacy principles and helping people make informed choices about sharing personal information, both within the organization and as part of service offerings.

As described in the section, the performance measurement process uses metrics to add, change or remove data points based on the ever-changing needs of the organization and stakeholders and impacts of external functions, such as laws, regulations and others. The Five-Step Metric Life Cycle provides the means to assist the privacy professional with identifying, defining, selecting, collecting and analyzing the appropriate metric data to satisfy the organization objectives and goals. The privacy professional should consider use of the life cycle as a standard practice to assist with metrics management and ensure sustainability.

Endnotes

1 Ian Glazer, *Maturity and Metrics: A few thoughts from the IAPP's Privacy Summit 2010*, www. tuesdaynight.org/tag/iappsummit.

2 Bob Blakley, *2010 Identity and Privacy Strategies Planning Guide: A Market in Transformation*. Burton Group, September 20, 2009.

3 Steve McConnell. *Software Estimation: Demystifying the Black Art*. Redmond, Wa.: Microsoft Press, 2006.

4 Knoernschild, Kirk. *Metrics: Improving IT Value, Justifying IT Investment*. Burton Group. Feb 23, 2009. PDF.

5 http://csrc.nist.gov/publications/nistir/ir7564/nistir-7564_metrics-research.pdf.

6 iSixSigma, *What is Six Sigma?* www.isixsigma.com/new-to-six-sigma/getting-started/what-six-sigma.

7 National Institute of Standards and Technology, Special Publication 800-55, revision 1,

"Performance Measurement Guide for Information Security," 32–33, http://csrc.nist.gov/publications/nistpubs/800-55-Rev1/SP800-55-rev1.pdf.

8   *Id.* at Appendix A, A-5–A-6.

9   The MITRE Corporation, *Cyber Resiliency Metrics,* Version 1.0, Rev. 1, April 2012, https://register.mitre.org/sr/12_2226.pdf.

10 Software Productivity Center Inc., *8-Steps Metric Program,* www.spc.ca/resources/metrics/8steps.htm.

11 Chris Schweighardt, *Calculating ROI to Realize Project Value,* March 27, 2010, www.isixsigma.com/operations/finance/calculating-roi-realize-project-value/.

12 Debra S. Herrmann, *Complete Guide to Security and Privacy Metrics: Measuring Regulatory Compliance, Operational Resilience and ROI,* 10, 2007, Auerbach Publications, Taylor & Francis Group, Boca Raton, FL.

13 *Id.*

14 Thomas R. Peltier, *Information Security Risk Analysis, Second Edition,* Auerbach Publications, Boca Raton, FL, 2005.

15 IBM, *Business Resilience: The Best Defense is a Good Offense: Develop a best practices strategy using a tiered approach,* 3, January 2009, www.ibm.com/smarterplanet/global/files/us__en_us__security_resiliency__buw03008usen.pdf.

16 *Id.*

17 Knoernschild *Metrics* at 8.

18 Davic C. Krehnke, "Corporate Governance: Information Security Essentials," Section 4. Sept 20, 2010. PDF.

19 *Id.*

20 Mike Neuenschwander, *Online Privacy and Regulatory Compliance: Improving Protection of Personal Information* 1 (Sep. 15, 2004).

PRIVACY OPERATIONAL LIFE CYCLE

A s discussed in Section I, privacy program governance provides a structured approach through two key high-level tasks and supporting subtasks.

This section addresses the privacy operational life cycle, using the details of privacy program governance to implement the operations management aspects of privacy through a four-phased privacy operational life cycle approach:

- Assess
- Protect
- Sustain
- Respond

The privacy operational life cycle is focused on refining and improving privacy processes, rather than a one-time effort. The privacy operational life cycle model continuously monitors and improves the privacy program, with the added benefits of a life cycle approach to measure (assess), improve (protect), evaluate (sustain) and support (respond), and then start again. As with all life cycle models, there is no particular entry point or exit point but instead a continuous cycle of improvement events related to privacy program operational management.

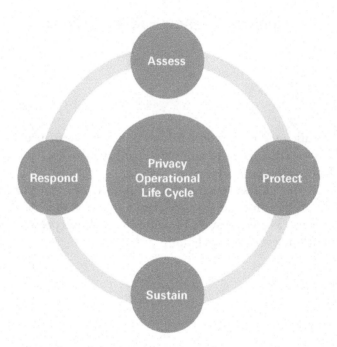

Figure II.2: Privacy Operational Life Cycle

Once the privacy program governance model is established using the strategic management, privacy strategy, and the structure of the privacy team, the privacy professional must then assess, protect, sustain, and respond to data privacy and the many management aspects necessary to protect that data. The assess phase of the model provides the framework for the privacy professional to evaluate the current processes, procedures, management, and practices for privacy management in the organization and apply best practices to them.

CHAPTER FOUR

Assess

"A ssess" is the first of four phases of the privacy operational life cycle that will
provide the steps, checklists and processes necessary to assess any gaps in a privacy
program as compared to industry best practices, corporate privacy policies,
applicable privacy laws and the privacy framework discussed in Section I of this book.
The privacy professional should note that although the assessing of a privacy program is
explained sequentially, in actual practice the elements may be performed simultaneously
or in separate components or tailored to organizational requirements. For example,
you may be assessing a program through measurement and alignment of organization
standards/guidelines and privacy management to regulatory and legislative mandates or
through industry best practices or a hybrid or combination of both approaches.

There are currently many models and frameworks that allow measurement and
alignment of these activities to include privacy maturity models, such as the American
Institute of Certified Public Accountants (AICPA) and the Canadian Institute of
Chartered Accountants (CICA) Maturity Model, Generally Accepted Privacy Principles
(GAPP) framework, EU Regulators Codes of Practice and Privacy by Design. Selection
and use should be based on the privacy framework found in Section I of this book.

1. Assessment Models

Using the privacy framework in the first section of this book, the privacy professional
should now understand frameworks and how to use them and their information to
establish all the privacy factors impacting the organization. Now the privacy professional
will need to map the established privacy requirements to the various activities and
processes that are associated with individual business functions. It is important to note
that in many organizations, these privacy requirements already exist in the organization's
corporate standards and guidelines. However, these requirements may require updating

to aligned jurisdictional and sectoral privacy laws. Maturity models are recognized methods by which organizations can measure progress against established benchmarks and measurements

The framework described in Section I is one example of a privacy framework. The privacy professional could use this or several other privacy industry maturity models, including the AICPA/CICA Privacy Maturity Model (PMM) and the Privacy by Design model. A maturity model provides a standardized reference for companies to use in assessing the level of maturity of their privacy programs. Each one is an excellent example of the methods and practices necessary to evaluate and grade the corporate risk. Once applied, any of these models will highlight the risk and lack of specific requirements or functions necessary for proper privacy program management.

The discussion that follows touches on representative areas within an organization. It is not intended to be exhaustive. Your organization may have different functions or areas that do not appear in this section, but you will find examples of how you can look at your organization's departments and functions as they relate to your privacy framework.

> *Don't use a sledge hammer to crack a walnut.* The maturity models discussed below are traditionally used by large multi-nationals and/or consultants engaged by global organizations and may seem unwieldy to smaller organizations with less privacy risk to manage. Remember, you do not need to follow any of the models exclusively. You can use some of just one, or bits from several. Make sure that the yardstick against which you are measuring your privacy program is fit for your purpose—the outputs of your review need to be capable of being meaningfully implemented within your organization. Privacy compliance is a journey; an effective assessment will guide you in what "next steps" you should take.

1.1 The AICPA/CICA Privacy Maturity Model

The AICPA/CICA Privacy Maturity Model (PMM) is an example of a well-known model used for over twenty years. It provides a very good and mature description of maturity levels: "Models are a recognized means by which organizations can measure their progress against established benchmarks."[1] Factors include:

- Becoming compliant is a journey, and progress along the way strengthens the organization, whether or not the organization has achieved all of the requirements

- In certain cases, such as security-focused maturity models, not every organization or every security application needs to be at the maximum for the organization to achieve an acceptable level of security

- Creation of values or benefits may be possible if they achieve a higher maturity level

Maturity models are a recognized means by which organizations can measure their progress against established benchmarks. —AICPA/CICA Privacy Maturity Model

The PMM uses five maturity levels:[2]

1. **Ad hoc.** Procedures or processes are generally informal, incomplete and inconsistently applied
2. **Repeatable.** Procedures or processes exist; however, they are not fully documented and do not cover all relevant aspects
3. **Defined.** Procedures and processes are fully documented and implemented and cover all relevant aspects
4. **Managed.** Reviews are conducted to assess the effectiveness of the controls in place
5. **Optimized.** Regular review and feedback are used to ensure continuous improvement towards optimization of the given process

Getting started with either example of maturity model, or even creating one of your own, can be done many ways. The AICPA/CICA PMM provides a structure to assist and identify where to start and what to document, as well as key start-up activities that include:[3]

- Identifying a project sponsor (chief privacy officer or equivalent)
- Appointing a project lead with sufficient privacy knowledge and authority to manage the project and assess the findings
- Forming an oversight committee that includes representatives from legal, human resources, risk management, internal audit, information technology and the privacy office
- Considering whether the committee requires outside privacy expertise
- Assembling a team to obtain and document information and perform the initial assessment of the maturity level
- Managing the project by providing status reports and the opportunity to meet and assess overall progress
- Providing a means to ensure that identifiable risk and compliance issues are appropriately escalated
- Ensuring the project sponsor and senior management are aware of all findings
- Identifying the desired maturity level by principle and/or for the entire organization for benchmarking purposes

These steps and many more can also be found in Chapter 2, Section 2.1, within the business case development steps. Accomplishing the maturity of the program provides the means to report the overall status for the return on investment (ROI) to the organization, as well as benchmarks to determine next steps to achieve a higher level of maturity. The privacy professional can use graphics, charts, written reports and other tools to benchmark the current status, while using those same tools to reflect improvements over time.

As the AICPA/CICA states, "In developing the PMM, it was recognized that each organization's personal information privacy practices may be at various levels, whether due to legislative requirements, corporate policies or the status of the organization's privacy initiatives. It was also recognized that, based on an organization's approach to risk, not all privacy initiatives would need to reach the highest level on the maturity model."[4]

An initial assessment can identify strengths and reveal weaknesses and gaps in your program. Areas needing attention might include deficiencies in technical controls or lack of training for employees; perhaps privacy requirements have not been fully integrated throughout all areas of the organization.

When a baseline assessment has been established, your organization can then decide at which level of maturity it ultimately wants or needs to operate. Not all organizations will need to operate at the highest level of maturity. Each organization should be intentional, though, in its commitment to increasing the maturity level of its privacy program.

1.2 Privacy by Design

Privacy by Design (PbD) is referenced in both Chapters 4 and 5 because the concept can be used to assess and/or protect, based on the needs of the organization. The privacy professional should assess the current organization objectives and goals to use PbD appropriately. PbD is a term developed by Dr. Ann Cavoukian, Information and Privacy Commissioner, Ontario, Canada, in the 1990s. PbD refers to the philosophy and approach of embedding privacy into the design of technology, business practices and physical design. Nymity is an ambassador for Privacy by Design focusing on business practices. Nymity created the privacy risk optimization process (PROP) to help organizations implement the philosophies of PbD into business practices.

The PbD framework dictates that privacy and data protection are embedded throughout the entire life cycle of technologies, from the early design stage to their deployment, use and ultimate disposal. The concept that organizations need to build privacy directly into technology, systems and practices at the design phase, thereby ensuring the existence of privacy from the outset, is the main principle.

1.2.1 Information and Privacy Commissioner, Ontario, Canada: Privacy by Design

"*Privacy by Design* (the Gold Standard for data protection), is *the* standard to be adopted for Smart Grid implementation for data protection. Embracing a positive-sum model whereby privacy and energy conservation may be achieved in unison is key to ensuring consumer confidence in electricity providers, as Smart Grid projects are initiated. Customer adoption and trust of Smart Grid energy savings programs is an integral factor in the success of energy conservation."[5]

*Read more about Privacy by Design on the Commissioner's website: www.ipc.on.ca/
english/Privacy/Introduction-to-PbD/*

1.2.2 U.S. Federal Trade Commission (FTC)

The FTC provides one example of a Privacy by Design implementation. "These
best practices [including Privacy by Design] can be useful to companies as they develop
and maintain processes and systems to operationalize privacy and data security practices
within their businesses." ... Privacy by Design's baseline principle is that] companies
should promote consumer privacy throughout their organizations and at every stage of
the development of their products and services to include:

A. The Substantive Principles: Companies should incorporate substantive privacy
   protections into their practices, such as data security, reasonable collection limits,
   sound retention and disposal practices, and data accuracy

B. Procedural Protections to Implement the Substantive Principles: Companies
   should maintain comprehensive data management procedures throughout the
   life cycle of their products and services"[6]

There are a number of specific areas where policy makers have a role in assisting
with the implementation of the self-regulatory principles that make up the final privacy
framework. Areas where the FTC is active:

1. Do not track

2. Mobile

3. Data brokers

4. Large platform providers

5. Promoting enforceable self-regulatory codes

Read more about FTC and Privacy by Design:
   1. www.ftc.gov/opa/2012/03/privacyframework.shtm
   2. http://ftc.gov/os/2012/03/120326privacyreport.pdf

1.2.3 IBM Corporation

The IBM Corporation provides another example of a Privacy by Design implementation.
For many organizations, Privacy Impact Assessments (PIAs) are manual, time-consuming
and labor-intensive projects. It can take a great deal of time to generate the questions
needed to identify privacy risk levels, conduct interviews, and review the answers collected.
Typically, a subject matter expert must analyze the answers to determine the privacy
risks and then summarize the findings and recommendations. Some organizations have

tried spreadsheet-based PIAs and have discovered that generating usable enterprise-level management reports is a daunting task. In practice, evaluating a single business process can require several weeks—or, at times, months—to determine its privacy risk.

"PIAs are, nonetheless, a vital tool when practicing PbD, for when they are properly implemented they provide important oversight to ensure privacy compliance. To enable the proactive use of PIA's throughout its global enterprise, IBM developed, over five years ago, a web-based Privacy Self-Assessment Tool that may be applied to any process or IT application within the organization."[7]

Identify and articulate your organization's aspirations. *So, you've identified which maturity model you are going to use (or part of one), but before you go any further you need to articulate (in one sentence or less) what your organization's privacy aspirations are: best in world, best in class, compliance with law, etc. Only when you can articulate where you want to be can a maturity model usefully illustrate to you how long the journey to get there is going to be. Think carefully about who in your organization needs to be consulted when articulating your privacy aspirations. For the vast majority of subject matter experts, privacy compliance is an overhead—a cost of doing business. Don't feel that your aspiration has to be "world class"; it is okay for your goal to be simply "to comply with all applicable data privacy laws in the jurisdictions within which we operate." Don't try and run before you can walk!*

2. Assess Key Areas of Your Business (Data, Systems and Process)

The functions of internal audit and risk management, information technology (IT), information security and privacy office/team are closely related and, in many companies, may form one team. A simple analogy may serve to describe this relationship. If you were to picture an information network in terms of plumbing, then IT would be directing attention to the pipes and how they fit together to allow for the proper flow of water (i.e., personal information). Internal audit/risk and information security, on the other hand, are more concerned with how securely the water flows through the pipes. They ask questions, such as: How can that water (data) be protected and who has access to it? Where does the water flow, which pipes are being used, and which pipes are inadvertently being exposed to wrong uses by wrong users (i.e., security breaches)?

A thorough privacy assessment approach should support these business areas.

- Internal audit and risk management
- Information technology: IT operations and development
  - Business continuity and disaster recovery planning

- Information security
  - Security, emergency services and physical access
  - Incident response and breach notification
- Human resources/ethics
- Legal and contracts
  - Compliance
  - Mergers, acquisitions and divestitures
- Processors and third-party vendor assessment
- Marketing/business development
- Government relations/public policy
- Finance/business controls

2.1 Internal Audit and Risk Management

Internal audit (IA) and risk management functions review and analyze the whole organization—all departments, functions and operations. They are responsible for discussing audit and risk with senior leaders, mid-level managers, first-level managers and employees. Based on the industry, these roles take on different meanings. Auditors and risk managers take on many roles and responsibilities based on the industry and organization, to include finance, performance, quality, project, operations and more. Their responsibilities include reviewing privacy assessment results and the identification of privacy risk for the organization.

Internal auditors evaluate the organization's risk management culture and identify risk factors within all systems, processes and procedures. In addition to evaluating control design and implementation to ensure proper risk management, internal auditors test those controls to ensure the proper operation. Risk managers ensure business and regulatory requirements through detailed market, credit, trade and counterparty analysis that communicate risk and issues throughout the organization.[8]

The nature of IA and risk management is different from other groups that may conduct internal risk assessments. Most IA departments report to an audit committee that reports to the board, assuming a predominantly independent role from the rest of the organization. While assessments come back with *recommendations* about what should be fixed, audits come back with findings that *must be* fixed. Since IA is independent of management in most cases (also a good best practice to separate the roles and responsibilities), the audit committee can be confident that internal audits are unbiased in the reporting of audit findings. Internal audits, or self audits, within an organization signify a commitment by the organization to be proactive in its approach to reducing corporate risk. This is evidenced by several positive contributions, such as:

- Focus on value-add activities beyond financial controls
- Use enterprise risk management (ERM) processes making risk a priority
- Hire auditors and risk managers with different skill sets (e.g. HR, IT, IA)
- Identify risk factors proactively, before they become incidents
- Ensure an independent perspective using audit committees and third parties on the governance, risk management, and control processes
- Identify and use best practices for recommendations to improve controls, performance, and reporting throughout the entire organization

2.2 Information Technology: IT Operations and Development

IT operations and development is a crucial piece of an organization's privacy program. Here is where the IT team implements controls and technical solutions in systems that include computers, networks and automated systems to provide a high degree of security technical controls in order to sustain the privacy program objectives and goals. It is important for IT operations and development to follow the organization's guidelines and incorporate privacy requirements from the outset.

There is no one-size-fits-all solution regarding technical controls—every environment has its own specific needs, requirements and protections. Smaller companies will not necessarily have the same kinds of security concerns that confront larger companies, so this area needs proper research and evaluation. The goal is always the same—to protect the data for every organization—so controls should be implemented through refined engineering processes that are repeatable, documented and measured.

Numerous technical controls, devices, systems and products exist throughout the market today. The privacy professional should leverage internal offices, such as IT or security, to assist in discussions, evaluations, requirements and use. A simple rule to follow with any technical issue is to use an expert rather than attempt to become an expert. Although privacy professionals may know and understand certain technologies, they should always consult, document and collaborate on all things IT and strengthen those ties to privacy.

2.2.1 Business Continuity and Disaster Recovery Planning

Although not typically thought of as a part of audit or risk, business continuity and disaster recovery planning (BCDR) are two complementary processes that prepare an organization for crises and managing the business afterwards, thereby reducing risk. As stated by an audit executive, "Internal audit's job is to provoke [thinking about] the unthinkable and ensure we have a plan."[9] The focus is to recover from a disaster when disruptions of any size are encountered. The overall goal of any BCDR plan is to maintain your organization's operations by mitigating the effects of disruptions. In other words, developing a good BCDR plan is practicing sound risk management.

BCDR is sometimes considered a high-cost insurance policy that is never used; thus the privacy professional should understand the key role played by this critical function and how it impacts (both negatively and positively) the organization. As the Info-Tech Research Group states, "When risk and business impact are misinterpreted or miscommunicated [within the BCDR plan], many problems arise:

- Lack of unified incident response across the organization
- Failure to achieve consensus on standardized recovery processes
- Incomplete or nonexistent risk assessments, assumptions and objectives
- Insufficient communication plans to coordinate recovery/continuity efforts
- Inability to recover data and applications"[10]

An effective BCDR ensures critical business functions continue; thus, understanding which staff and systems are mandatory to continue as a business and how to resume operations are necessary components. Recovery and restoration of personal information must be handled appropriately during the recovery period. The stressful conditions experienced during disaster recovery operations can cause mistakes that result in data being exposed. It is essential, therefore, to have a plan in place prior to a crisis to safeguard all personal information that ensures the organization privacy objectives and goals. Info-Tech recommends the following BCDR practices:[11]

- Make BCDR clear to executives so they understand BCDR is more than technology and must be properly budgeted and tested
- Convince the business to get involved so they understand the cost of downtime in lost business, customer relationships and customer service
- Develop recovery time objectives and recovery point objectives and then communicate those throughout the organization to stakeholders at all levels to ensure collaboration, support and awareness
- Use BCDR best practices; do not create the wheel, and eliminate rework or duplicated work between IT, security and privacy

Because the BCDR plans include many components, the privacy professional should focus on the privacy aspects to protect and manage data privacy throughout BCDR planning, execution and reporting. As an example, during a pandemic, Rachel Hayward states, "Privacy professionals need to work with the business continuity planners and human resource departments to clarify any questions regarding the collection, use, and disclosure of personal employee information during the development of organizational [business continuity plans] that include considerations … The challenge is to balance these needs with the needs of the organization to plan for the potential of prolonged staff shortages caused by employee illness, and, potentially, employees staying home from work to care for loved ones ... a single department within an organization may be severely affected while other areas are less affected, or not affected at all."[12]

The privacy professional should ask the following questions for BCDR:

- Does our BCDR plan align with our organization's privacy policies and procedures?
- How will we protect personal information from loss and exposure before, during and after an event?
    - Maintaining a backup system off-site?
    - Training for backup employees to handle various tasks in an emergency?
- Are there business contingency plans in place that ensure data privacy?
    - Alternate locations for office operations with the same protections?
    - Alternate means of communicating within the organization and to outside contacts (e.g. supply chain networks, customers) with the same level of privacy controls?

It is recommended the BCDR be assessed from a privacy perspective.

2.3 Information Security

Information security is a complex topic that includes technical and physical controls that span the organization to form IT systems, building security, remote users, vendors and third parties. As controls change all the time based on newer releases of technology, software applications, upgrades, decommissions and rotation in staff, control management should be an agenda item at many privacy and security meetings to communicate, understand and provide proper management practices, information and collaboration of that data. These controls have to include the privacy requirements of the organization.

As privacy is concerned with an individual's ability to control the use of personal information, information security focuses on mechanisms for protection of information and information systems.

At the high level, information security provides standards and guidelines for applying management, technical and operational controls to reduce the probable damage, loss, modification or unauthorized access to systems, facilities or data. This includes having a strategy for document destruction, sanitization of hard drives and portable drives, security of fax machines, imaging and copier machines. Many times there is confusion between applying all three of these controls, and information security is only considered within the technical controls of an enterprise, domain, system, etc. The privacy professional should become an expert with all three as related to the policies, standards and codes of conduct of the organization's management structure, objectives and goals.

At the highest levels, these three controls are secured through three common information security principles from the 1960s, known as the C-I-A triad, or information security triad:

- **Confidentiality.** Prevention of unauthorized disclosure of information
- **Integrity.** Ensure information is protected from unauthorized or unintentional alteration, modification or deletion
- **Availability.** Information is readily accessible to authorized users

Further advanced information security concepts developed years after the principles from above were established include:

- **Accountability.** Entity ownership is traceable
- **Assurance.** All other four objectives are met

These practices apply high-level reasoning to risk management and define the organization's objectives and goals for data security. Since security practices are based on geographical, legal, regulatory and other considerations, the privacy professional should understand the organizational strategies to meet those and determine stakeholders for communication, collaboration and information sharing. Information security in general is a complex topic that may span the organization. By becoming familiar with the stakeholders, the privacy professional will have open channels of communication to and from those key players throughout the life cycle management aspects.

It is important the security controls are an integral part of the privacy assessment process.

2.3.1 Security, Emergency Services and Physical Access

All security-related services should be aligned with the organization's privacy policies and procedures. Physical security measures implemented at each facility should reflect the sensitivity of the information housed at that location. Procedures should be in place to control access to the organization's facilities and to prevent unauthorized access to resources within those facilities.

Monitoring physical access to the organization's facilities is a function of the security department. Procedures should be in place to confirm that the data being used to monitor access (e.g., surveillance videos, access logs, etc.) is handled, stored and destroyed appropriately, in accordance with the entity's privacy and security requirements. The security department should also be aware of the organization's incident response protocol, as they may be required to notify or otherwise provide evidence of potential breaches to the designated parties (e.g., privacy office, incident response team, information security, etc.) and to help support investigations regarding unauthorized access or compromise. It is also important these services, wherever they collect personal information, also undergo a privacy assessment.

2.4 Human Resources/Ethics

Depending on the organization's size, industry, geographical location and more, HR and ethics management cross boundaries or are totally separate. Smaller organizations might be forced to merge the offices, while larger organizations could devote many more resources to these tasks.

2.4.1 Human Resources

Staff in the HR department looks at the personal information life cycle of specific HR data to ensure that the handling of all information by HR personnel is in compliance with the organization's privacy policies and procedures.

The human resources function will include personal information in areas such as:

- Talent acquisition and hiring
- Performance management
- Training and development
- Compensation and benefits
- Employee relations
- Employee records
- Succession planning

Multinational organizations are required to meet local regulations and the privacy expectations of their employees in all countries in which they operate. Obligations do not simply disappear because the office or employees are in another state, country or continent. Specifically, cross-border data transfers should be monitored to regulate the export of personal data to ensure regulatory compliance and data privacy. The employment contract provides overall employee consent for certain work-related activities. Some surveillance/monitoring in the workplace will require additional privacy considerations.

Employee privacy considerations are other important activities for HR to review:

- Investigations of fraud and criminal activities
- Handling of organization trade secrets for the protection of that information
- Prevention of discrimination, sexual harassment and other human rights concerns
- Compliance with workplace safety
- System integrity with compliance of security and privacy practices[13]

2.4.2 Ethics

Not all companies have a separate ethics office, but all companies need to have an ethics function. This may be tied in with compliance or HR, but there needs to be accountability for people doing the right thing within the organization.

There needs to be a trusted place in your organization where people can take their complaints, concerns and possible whistle blowing when necessary. If an allegation should arise, for example, concerning someone invading another individual's personal information, there needs to be a procedure for responding, resolving and documenting the situation. Usually this is a function of the privacy office.

Ethics will often function in a manner similar to IA; that is, independent of the normal chain of command and properly empowered and staffed to perform necessary tasks. Ethics will usually report directly to the board, or as close to the board as possible. This is necessary to guard the integrity of the ethics function, protect the data and protect the organization from possible misconceptions of data confidentially. If an allegation were to be made against the chief executive officer of the corporation, for instance, you could not have your ethics department reporting to the very person being investigated. By guarding the independent operations of the ethics function, your organization sends a strong message about its commitment to privacy protection.

Wherever the ethics function is located within your organization, you need to make sure that you are addressing the issue of people doing the right thing with other people's personal information, investigating matters as they arise and reporting those to proper stakeholders to protect the individuals and the organization.

2.5 Legal and Compliance

As with many other categories, legal and contracts can overlap in layers or be two distinct topics, depending on the organization's size, geographical location and other factors. These tasks may overlap within administrative, clerical and research duties.

> *Legal, security, audit, risk and compliance may overlap or be separate based on the organization.*

2.5.1 Legal

"Privacy policies have become long legal documents that most attorneys, let alone the average consumer, have difficulty understanding. They are meant to provide notice to individuals about data collection, use and disclosure policies. However, they are often complicated, long, and unintelligible and, as a result, rarely read by the average consumer … Your organization's privacy practices must align with its privacy promises to minimize legal liability. You can do so by conducting factual and legal due diligence. The factual due diligence allows you to determine what information your organization uses. The legal due diligence allows you to determine what laws govern the use of that information. You need to understand both in order to competently draft a privacy policy that minimizes legal risk for your organization."[14] The legal office is therefore the necessary owner of this task, to perform legal liability activities in conducting the due diligence.

To perform this due diligence, a legal office, team or person with the legal roles, responsibilities and empowerment must be appointed to act for the organization. This role will then have the responsibility for ensuring that the organization is in compliance with all legislative, regulatory and market requirements that are specific to your industry. They should also understand local privacy obligations and requirements that pertain to that organization in the countries from which the data is collected. This includes, for example, registering and obtaining international transfer approvals with data protection authorities (DPA) in those countries where this is required.

Administrative, clerical and research duties may apply across the organization or be delegated to a small group. Administrative duties may include legal advice, translation of laws and regulations into plain language, lawsuits, and senior leadership to the organization. Clerical duties include contracts (e.g., assisting the contracts office, writing contracts, etc.), legal document management and possible budget and expenditure assistance.

Research is another legal duty to ensure the organization is acting in accordance with laws, regulations, industry, geographical location, etc. The privacy professional should become familiar with the legal staff and how the organization performs the legal duties, as well as how privacy is impacted, managed, addressed, and considered or *scrutinized* by the legal team.

Legal should have controls, documentation management practices and tracking mechanisms to identify, track and record all procurements, contacts, service-level agreements and performance measurements for privacy management. Are there established procedures in place, for instance, to review contracts with vendors who handle personal data while representing your business? Is that data tracked and reviewed on an ongoing basis? Do the organization customers have a need to review this material for auditing or reporting purposes? The vendors must be held to the same standards as employees, and all vendor functions must be aligned to the privacy requirements you've established through your privacy framework.

An incident management and breach response team should include IT, security, the privacy office, legal and HR as required. This team manages the breach notification activities, as necessary, with guidance and leadership from the legal office to ensure understanding of the regulatory aspects and internal control of the information, the findings and the impacts that result. The legal office—as a privacy management stakeholder—should be aware of the privacy governance in the organization, roles and responsibilities, lines of communication, joint planning and coordination of risk.

2.5.2 Compliance

Privacy compliance is no less complicated than the legal aspects. For example, in the EU, the EU Data Protection Directive requires member states to adopt laws that protect personal information, to disclose who is collecting the data and why, and who will ultimately have access to it. The Directive also gives the person the right to access the data and make corrections to it. Some multinational organizations doing business between the EU and U.S. may use Safe Harbor, while companies operating solely with the U.S. have federal, state and local regulations and laws that are sectoral, based within finance, healthcare and other industries. Compliance to the privacy standards and laws is challenging and not getting any easier. As stated in Chapter 2, because penalties for violation of privacy laws and regulations are increasing, the privacy professional must be prepared to address, track and understand any penalty that could affect the organization.

> *Compliance to privacy standards and laws is challenging and not getting any easier, regardless of geographic location, industry or organization size.*

Compliance can exist within any of the core business functions: legal, security, IT, audit or others. There are specific merits to the layering, overlapping or separation of each as defined by the organization objectives or goals. Regardless, the roles and responsibilities of each function must still be performed in one way or another to ensure the success of the organization. Mark Ruppert states that the advantages and disadvantages of combining these include:

- Separation of legal, compliance, internal audit and security functions: "collaboration is more challenging, but functional independence is assured."
- Combining legal, compliance, internal audit and security functions: "collaboration is assured, but functional independence is more challenging."[15]

He also highlighted the fact that twenty-two comparative compliance categories exist within a *generic* organization to reflect the complexity in the compliance roles and responsibilities that may include:[16]

- Requirement
- Purpose
- Reporting
- Internal authority
- Span of responsibility
- Professional standards
- High-level focus
- Primary risk focus

- Activity focus
- Relationship management
- Training
- Auditing
- Monitoring
- Expertise
- Compliance plan

- Risk
- Follow-up
- Investigation
- Hotline
- Information systems
- Internal controls
- And others that overlap from this list

Access to the organization, proper governance, lines of reporting and authority, organization placement and organizational access impact all of these categories to achieve effective privacy management and governance. The privacy professional will need to define the roles and responsibilities of compliance for the organization and document when, where and how privacy is managed within many of these layers. The starting point to complete this task may be within several offices or unique roles that depend greatly on the organizational structure and purpose. It may be the legal office, internal audit, risk management or privacy office itself.

Because of the overlap for compliance, the privacy professional should be prepared to track and investigate all possible roles and responsibilities within the organization. Remember that each organization completes this role differently by combining or separating them. The key will always be found in the organizational governance structure, joint planning and coordination of risk management in the organization. Risk is typically the driving factor for establishment of many offices, including privacy, security, audit and compliance, so the starting point will be to understand the organizational risk approach, the supporting offices and the governance.

2.5.3 Mergers, Acquisitions and Divestitures

Mergers, acquisitions and divestitures contain many legal and compliance aspects, with their own sets of concerns related to privacy. Mergers form one organization from others, while acquisitions involve one organization buying one or many others; divestitures remove one aspect of an organization for several motives, which may include selling off part of the business not integral to the core.

An organization can be exposed to unnecessary corporate risk by acquiring companies that may have different regulatory concerns than the current business environment. Examples below illustrate the need to consider the variety of regulatory considerations that may be involved in any of these actions, to include:

- Acquiring an organization that is a U.S. Health Insurance Portability and Accountability Act (HIPAA)-covered entity if the parent organization is not

- Acquiring an organization that needs to meet PCI-compliant standards or other regulatory compliance, such as Statement on Auditing Standards, No. 70, Service Organizations (SAS 70) reporting

- Acquiring an organization that has employees in countries with specific privacy legislation; for example, PIPEDA, EU Data Protection Directive, etc.

- The acquisition of an organization with existing client agreements requires a review by the new ownership in regards to the control, movement and use of the data, including marketing

- New resources, technologies and processes need to be assessed in order to identify all actions that are required to bring them into alignment with privacy and security policies before they are integrated into the existing system

2.5.3.1 Divestitures

With respect to both partial and total divestitures, the organization should conduct a thorough assessment of the infrastructure of all, or any part of, the entity being divested prior to the conclusion of the divestiture. These activities are performed to confirm that no unauthorized sensitive information, including personal information, remains on the organization's infrastructure as part of the divestiture, with the exception of any pre-approved proprietary data.

It is important to the organization to include a privacy checkpoint as part of the merger, acquisition, and divestiture processes.

2.6 Processors and Third-Party Vendor Assessment

Processors, third-party vendors and business process outsourcers who are now a part of the standardized business practice must also be part of the privacy management program to remain vigilant about data protection. In the majority of the legislations, accountability remains with the organization; therefore, privacy controls that determine how data is to be protected and handled must exist in the contracts with the processors and third-party vendors. Compliance factors, the ever-changing landscape of privacy and security regulations, multinational considerations, geographical location and other factors relevant to storing, processing, and transmitting privacy data must maintained.

Organizations should carefully vet vendors prior to selection and continue to monitor and audit them through the life of the contract to ensure proper privacy and security risk management practices. Contract language should be written to call out privacy protections and regulatory requirements within the statement of work and then mapped to service-level agreements to ensure there are no questions about the data privacy responsibilities, breach response, incident response, media press releases on breaches, possible fines, and other considerations, as if the vendor were part of the organization. Privacy/security questionnaires, privacy impact assessments and other checklists can be used to assess the vendor risk and should include consideration for the vendor's privacy and information security policies, access controls, where the personal information will be held and who has access to it. Results may indicate improvement areas that may be fixed or identify higher-level risk that may limit the ability of that vendor to properly perform privacy protections.

Once risk is determined, the organization best practices may also be leveraged to assist a vendor too small in size or with other limited resources by offering security engineering, risk management, training through awareness and education, auditing and others.

The vendor contract should include specific information about what services the vendor will be providing and what the vendor's responsibilities are. The following list gives a few examples of the kind of information you may want to consider including:

- Specifying the type of personal information the vendor will have access to at remote locations
- How the vendor plans to protect personal information
- The vendor's responsibilities in the event of a data breach
- How the data will be disposed of when the contract is terminated
- Limitations on the use of data that ensure that it only be used for specified purposes
- Rights of audit and investigation
- Liability for data breach

The purpose of the vendor contract is to make certain that all vendors are in compliance with the requirements of your organization's privacy program.

2.7 Marketing/Business Development

Aligning marketing/business development means that any activities where information is collected and shared as a function of marketing must conform to regulatory privacy practices.

2.8 Finance/Business Controls

Finance is linked to many of the other organizational functions discussed in this chapter. Finance will typically control the money and budget of an organization, including employee payroll, investments, expenditures and many other sensitive key business indicators that may or may not be within the scope of privacy. Financial functions should align with requirements in the privacy framework and legal, security, risk and many other governance factors of the organization. Internal lines of communication and control are necessary to establish and observe privacy practices to ensure organizational objectives and goals.

Finance must have some effective means to track any changes to regulatory requirements and to update finance employees' awareness of those changes. All financial functions must handle financial information that aligns with current regulatory requirements) and the overall privacy program.

Examples of financial functions include:

- Accounts receivable
- Accounts payable
- Payroll
- Securities
- Investments

Don't be reluctant to phone a friend. Conducting a gap analysis using some or all of someone else's maturity model is not necessarily an intuitive activity. Professionals usually study and pass exams in their chosen subject fields—it takes time to become proficient. If you've never conducted a review before, ask relevant and experienced colleagues for help and advice. The IA function may have templates you can adapt and use. You may be lucky, and they may offer to partner with you in conducting the assessment. Use the internal resources and skills available to you; they know your business best. You don't necessarily have to hire expensive internal consultants.

All processes in the above functions should undergo a privacy assessment if/when personal information is handled.

3. Summary

Assessment of your organization's privacy program is one stage of the privacy operational life cycle. There are a variety of models and frameworks—including maturity models— that provide guidelines for measuring and aligning privacy activities. These models can be used in whole or in part to help your organization conduct an effective assessment.

Endnotes

1   AICPA/CICA, Privacy Maturity Model, March 2011, www.aicpa.org/InterestAreas/ InformationTechnology/Resources/Privacy/DownloadableDocuments/10-229_AICPA_ CICA%20Privacy%20Maturity%20Model_FINALebook_revised0612.pdf.

2   *Id.* at 2.

3   *Id.* at 3.

4   *Id.* at 2.

5   Information and Privacy Commissioner, *Executive Summary*, www.ipc.on.ca/site_documents/ achieve-goldstnd_execsumm.pdf.

6   Federal Trade Commission, *Protecting Consumer Data in an Era of Rapid Change: Recommendations for Businesses and Policy Makers*, p.iii, p. vii, March 2012, http://ftc.gov/ os/2012/03/120326privacyreport.pdf.

7   Information and Privacy Commissioner, Ontario, Canada, *Privacy by Design: From Policy to Practice*, September 2001, www.ipc.on.ca/images/Resources/pbd-policy-practice.pdf.

8   Counterparty: commonly used in the financial services industry to describe a legal entity, unincorporated entity or collection of entities to which an exposure to financial risk might exist.

9   Ernst & Young, *Executive Summary: Internal Audits Evolving Role: A Proactive Catalyst of Business Improvement* (2011), www.energycollection.us/Board-Of-Directors/Audit/Internal-Audits-Evolving.pdf.

10 Ross Armstrong, Info-Tech Research Group, "Draw the line between DRP and Business Continuity," (April 22, 2008), http://blog.infotech.com/research/draw-the-line-between-drp-and-business-continuity/.

11 *Id.*

12 Rachel Hayward. "Privacy and pandemic planning: a few prudent considerations for organizations," January 1, 2010, www.privacyassociation.org/publications/2010_01_01_privacy_and_pandemic_planning_a_few_prudent_considerations.

13 International Chamber of Commerce. *Employee privacy, data protection and human resources*, http://intgovforum.org/Substantive_1st_IGF/Employee.privacy.data%20protection.and.human.resources.pdf.

14 Mehmet Menur, Sarah Branam and Matt Mrkobrad. *Best practices in drafting plain-language and layered privacy policies*, September 01, 2012, www.privacyassociation.org/publications/2012_09_01_best_practices_in_drafting_plain_language_and_layered_privacy_po.

15 Mark Ruppert. *Contrasting Roles and Responsibilites—Corporate Compliance and Internal Audit*, 25 (2006). Associate of Healthcare Internal Auditors. New Perspectives.

16 *Id.*

CHAPTER FIVE

Protect

review 105 - 110
pp

"Protect" is the second of four phases of the privacy operational life cycle. It provides the *data life cycle, information security practices and Privacy by Design* principles to "protect" personal information. Although technical, containing information security, information assurance or cyber security practices, this chapter provides a generic, high-level overview for the privacy professional. The protect phase of the privacy operational life cycle embeds privacy principles and information security management practices within the organization to address, define, and establish privacy practices.

For any organization, domestic and global privacy management is further complemented through each of the operational life cycle phases related to jurisdiction, compliance and laws. Understanding and analyzing each of these phases as they relate to an organization provides the privacy professional a greater understanding of how to protect personal information.

> *Privacy cuts across the entire organization, from HR, legal and other supporting functions to businesses and procurement. Therefore, do not forget to take into account laws and regulations applying to other areas (such as labor or telecommunications law), as these may well interact with privacy laws.*

1. Data Life Cycle Management (DLM) *review this*

Data life cycle management (DLM), also known as information life cycle management (ILM) or data governance, is a policy-based approach to managing the flow of information through a life cycle from creation to final disposition. DLM provides a holistic approach to the processes, roles, controls and measures necessary to organize and maintain data.

DLM can also be considered a mitigation that is aimed at lowering the risk of data breaches by reducing the volume and type of data stored. A well-written and well-planned DLM strategy provides data-handling policy reviews for types of data, processing activities, storage, sharing and data destruction, as well as setting forth employee roles and responsibilities for each stage of the process.[1]

1.1 The Need for DLM

DLM has become increasingly more complex. For example, compliance requirements for U.S., EU and Japanese laws change and complicate business record retention and auditing requirements. U.S. laws, such as the Sarbanes-Oxley Act (SOX), the Health Insurance Portability and Accountability Act (HIPAA) and the Internal Revenue Code, along with the EU laws through the 8th Company Law Directive on Statutory Audit (Directive 2006/43/EC) (E-SOX) and Japan's Financial Instruments and Exchange Law (J-SOX), all establish data retention and reporting requirements. Each set of requirements further complicates compliance efforts because they are not products but comprehensive approaches to managing an organization's data that involve polices, roles, responsibilities, procedures and best practices, in conjunction with applications and other security and technical controls.

> *In large organizations, the DLM allows for identification and timely address of possible issues stemming from conflict of laws and differences in compliance with local legislation. Indeed, one of the challenges for a good DLM is the ability to recognize a problem before it becomes an emergency.*

The need for DLM has also grown out of organizations' desire to "cull" the volume and type of information stored or kept. Unlike the old days, when the filing cabinets would overflow and provide an obvious visual cue—drawers that won't close or paper falling on the floors—there is no visual electronic indicator or natural physical limitation to file storage in the new digital age. Electronic storage is simple and cheap. Warehouses full of documents can now be stored on computers no bigger than a desktop personal computer or a removable drive. As a result, rather than manage paper files, we have become a society of hoarders—keeping everything digital.

1.2 Data Life Cycle Management Principles

The potential liability can be mitigated by creating data life cycle management policies and procedures to limit data collection. Saving too much data or too little data can have consequences for the organization; thus, DLM practices will define those based on the needs of the organization.

"**Information governance** is the specification of decision rights and an accountability framework to encourage desirable behavior in the valuation, creation, storage, use, archival and deletion of information. It includes the processes, roles, standards and metrics that ensure the effective and efficient use of information in enabling an organization to achieve its goals."[2]

Governance (of anything) consists of several elements, the most fundamental of which are decision rights and accountability. In the area of information governance, for example, one might question who decides how long a particular data set is kept. Decisions can be made by individuals or groups. Once those decisions are made—for example, in the context of an e-mail retention policy—we can then ask, "Who is held accountable for enforcing the decision?" Sometimes it's easy. As in the e-mail example, if a organization and its IT department decide to retain e-mail on the Exchange server for only 90 days, individual users have little recourse; messages more than 90 days old can be automatically deleted. The IT organization can be held accountable for enforcing the policy.

Governance also consists of processes and standards (*how this will be managed*) and roles (*who will manage*). A goal of an effective governance strategy is to ensure that information assets adequately support business objectives. First, a decision must be made as to what information assets are worth the investment, from a governance perspective. Too much time and effort are wasted on creating and maintaining information that is of little to no value to the business, such as duplicate copies of files, old and outdated information and so on.

As James Short states, "The main drivers of ILM [and DLM] are: enterprise data growth; growth in unstructured data; limitations in relational database management system performance; information access and security concerns; lack of effective methods for classifying data; and difficulty in assessing productivity of systems, applications and databases. The main benefits cited of ILM [and DLM] are increased control over data, regulatory compliance (thereby minimizing business risk), and reduced costs (by eliminating redundancies in data storage)."[3]

The 11-element DLM model is based on George L. Paul and Robert F. Copple's seven basic principles of electronic data life cycle policy:[4]

1. ***Enterprise Objectives.*** To reduce the "save everything" plan, the organization must first understand the "objectives" in maintaining its electronic records. Data have many different degrees of importance and sensitivity; thus, information must be categorized by order of magnitude in the organization. "Accordingly, the first job is to prioritize. What is critical for the business? Devise information life cycle management with such critical records in mind."[5]

2. ***Minimalism.*** Discard all data unless a good business (or legal) reason exists to maintain that data. Review the data collected and the regulatory constraints. Preserve data only if relevant to "ongoing or foreseeable litigation, now known as the Zubulake standard. The overall goal is to comply with law and to achieve business objectives, but not to save data that is not required by law or for business purposes."[6]

3. ***Simplicity of Procedure and Effective Training.*** Ensure that the approach to process, data life cycle and policy development delivers requirements, controls and guidance that are clear and easy to implement and follow. Not all privacy professionals are lawyers or involved in legal standards. Policy documents, training materials, etc., should be easy to read and understand, relevant to the

intended audience and provide points of contact for questions. "As with all things corporate, there is a strong tendency for policy initiatives to become increasingly intricate to the point of dysfunction (only interpretable by those with graduate degrees in operations research). Once the policy becomes too complex, it is virtually guaranteed that employees will simply ignore it."[7]

4. *Adequacy of Infrastructure.* The organization systems must be able to support the task and requirements, from a technical standpoint. "It is, indeed, often astounding how 'out-of-scale' an organization's infrastructure is to accomplish appropriate data management. Here, as elsewhere, teamwork between higher management and IS workers is critical. Hardware is seldom the problem. The problem is the software and human systems infrastructure relating to information security; access control; authenticity; retrievability and auditability."[8]

5. *Information Security.* This is an essential piece of DLM. Cross-functional efforts that include Information Security personnel during the development, implementation and maintenance of a DLM framework or strategy will not only ensure the implementation of appropriate technical controls necessary to protect organization information assets but will also provide additional depth and awareness across various parts of the organization.

6. *Authenticity and Accuracy of One's Own Records.* "Give thought to how one might prove the authenticity of one's own records if they are ever challenged in court, an administrative proceeding, or an audit. This suggests the need for proactive procedures. Authenticity, which has been stretched to the breaking point by the new information paradigm, should no longer be taken for granted."[9]

7. *Retrievability.* "[O]ne of the hallmarks of the metamorphosis from a document/record/file keeping culture to a culture of data multiplying on a shared networked, edited by many and stored on scalable media" is the ability to quickly index, search and retrieve data.[10] Designing this capability into the DLM framework from the start can enable effortless accessibility and retrievability. If using a database, discuss the plans with a database architect. Engaging multiple subject matter experts early in the planning and design phases in, for example, the areas of engineering services and database architecture, will provide a broader perspective and lead to more useful, thorough implementation of the data life cycle management framework. "Law firms, strange to say, are in the vanguard of businesses in this respect. Their handling of huge numbers of different types of electronic files for many different customers has led to databases that facilitate filing by subject matter, with automatic indexing, and easy retrievability. This 'subject matter centered' database control of data has yet to make it into the mainstream of businesses' data storage … Don't be penny wise and pound foolish."[11]

8. *Distribution Controls.* Data can now be transmitted within seconds around the globe. "Once the digital genie is out of the electronic bottle, no amount of wishing can contain it. Every day there are new examples of this phenomenon."[12] Business data can be controlled with access controls; however, there are always the issues of insider threats, employee errors and mishaps unrelated to any pre-planned activity. E-mail mistakes, lost backup tapes, and files stored in an unprotected file share by mistake may all lead to the same unfortunate outcome: possible disaster. "One solution is to employ one of the available software solutions that encrypt the data and allow the sender to specify the degree of republication rights granted to the recipient. Sophisticated companies are beginning to utilize these types of solutions as part of their overall data management strategy."[13]

9. *Auditability.* "Unless the Data Life Cycle Management system can pass an audit, an organization is put in an unfortunate situation indeed. Along these lines, all companies should seriously consider the use of 'hashing,' 'digital signatures,' and logging of network events to provide a framework of 'testability' for the information flowing in their ecosystem at any point in time."[14]

10. *Consistency of Policies.* Data retention policies within the DLM framework should be consistently implemented; otherwise, it may appear the organization may have the intention of wrongdoing. Multinational and multi-sector organizations have an additional challenge to ensure polices are as consistent and uniform for the organization between locations, yet meet local laws, regulations and industry guidance. Different parts of the business may have different data retention polices; thus, the organization should document and review as necessary. Inconsistency between these should be explained fully to ensure there are no gaps or misunderstandings. Consistent execution of the DLM plan in all circumstances reflects better on the organization and will not draw questions of wrongdoing. "If there are dates or milestones for data review and disposal, they should be adhered to" without question or waivers.[15]

11. *Enforcement.* This must also be simple, consistent and accurate throughout the DLM framework, ensuring the organization complies with internally dictated policies and practices. Consistent enforcement also may motivate employees to do the right thing, as they will always know the consequences of noncompliance.[16]

Establishing and maintaining the DLM framework is not a one-time process but should become part of an organization's ecosystem for proper electronic records management. "The advent of electronic data storage and digital communications has provided business, consumers, and the public with untold benefits, including access to vast amounts of information and incredible speed in analysis and distribution. Implementing and maintaining a data life cycle management system is a small, but necessary, price to pay for continuing to be a player in the marketplace."[17] Addressing the DLM through implementation of these 11 fundamental principles will allow for the proper management of:

- Records retention
- Data privacy
- Data security
- Data breach
- Data transfer
- Media/format
- Storage
- e-Discovery
- Lawful access
- Internal investigations

2. Information Security Practices

Information security and privacy practices exist within a mutual space of data protection. Security aims to ensure the confidentiality, integrity and availability of data as stored, transmitted and used, while privacy addresses the rights of individuals to control how and to what extent information about them—their personal information—is collected and further processed. The paradox created by the intersection of security measures and the concept of civil privacy liberties, or privacy "rights," results in various concerns, depending on an individual's view or personal beliefs. Within the United States, specifically, following the September 11, 2001 terrorist attack, public insecurity and fear led to the prioritization of security over the protection of individual privacy. Many people, however, still expect and require that their privacy interests, or perceived privacy rights, will be protected. This paradox can frustrate the privacy professional, who must rationalize civil liberties and privacy rights with the demands of laws, regulations and industries for *both* privacy and security. Since these terms are rarely defined and often confused when used, the privacy professional must understand each concept individually and their interactions and intersections.

Information security is built upon risk management practices to provide:

- Identification of risk
- Selection and implementation of measures to mitigate risks
- Tracking and evaluation of risk to validate the first two parts

Regardless of industry, government affiliation or geographic location, risk factors are the driving force behind all information security matters. Because of the uncertainty of future risk losses, perfect security implies zero loss, which is infinitely expensive and thus almost impossible to achieve. Enterprises, systems, applications and other technologies will always have security risk; but the existence of risk does not necessarily imply they are not secure. Instead, risk is identified, controls are selected and implemented, and risk is tracked based on pre-defined severity categories. For example:

- U.S. financial laws, such as the Sarbanes–Oxley Act (SOX), HIPAA and the Internal Revenue Code, along with the EU laws through the 8th Company Law Directive on Statutory Audit (Directive 2006/43/EC) (E-SOX) and Japan's Financial Instruments and Exchange Law (J-SOX), demand risk management practices.

- The U.S. government calls this "Security Engineering through Information Assurance Management," which includes intrusion detection, incident response, engineering, certification and accreditation, etc., via a risk management framework as directed by the Federal Information Security Management Act (FISMA), the Office of Management and Budget (OMB), HIPAA and others.

- International standards applying similar risk management principles through such principles as the ISO/IEC 27000 series provide best-practice recommendations on information security management, risks and controls within the context of an overall information security management system (ISMS), similar in design to management systems for quality assurance (the ISO 9000 series) and environmental protection (the ISO 14000 series).[18] This includes:

  - **ISO/IEC 27000.** Information security management systems—Overview and vocabulary
  - **ISO/IEC 27001.** Information security management systems—Requirements
  - **ISO/IEC 27002.** Code of practice for information security management
  - **ISO/IEC 27003.** Information security management system implementation guidance
  - **ISO/IEC 27004.** Information security management—Measurement
  - **ISO/IEC 27005.** Information security risk management
  - **ISO/IEC 27006.** Requirements for bodies providing audit and certification of information security management systems
  - **ISO/IEC 27010.** Information technology, security techniques, information security management for inter-sector and inter-organizational communications

- **ISO/IEC 27011.** Information security management guidelines for telecommunications organizations based on ISO/IEC 27002
- **ISO/IEC 27031.** Guidelines for information and communications technology readiness for business continuity
- **ISO/IEC 27033-1.** Network security overview and concepts
- **ISO/IEC 27035.** Information security incident management
- **ISO 27799.** Information security management in health using ISO/IEC 27002

- Once the risk management framework is determined, information security provides management, technical and operational controls to reduce probable damage, loss, modification or unauthorized data access. Confusion may exist as to the distinction between technical, management and operational controls. Often, security controls are perceived as *only* technical in nature, applied within the enterprise, domain, system, etc. The privacy professional should become familiar with all three as related to the policies, standards and laws of the organization's management structure, governance, objectives and goals.

As mentioned in Chapter 4, these three types of controls are viewed through three common information security principles from the 1960s, known as the C-I-A triad, or information security triad:

- **Confidentiality.** Prevention of unauthorized disclosure of information
- **Integrity.** Ensures information is protected from unauthorized or unintentional alteration, modification or deletion
- **Availability.** Information is readily accessible to authorized users

Additional advanced concepts not used all the time include:

- **Accountability.** Entity ownership is traceable
- **Assurance.** All other four objectives are met

These principles apply high-level reasoning to risk management and define the objectives and goals necessary to data security. Practically every information security standard today is premised on these core principles in standards development efforts. The U.S. National Institute of Standards and Technology (NIST), Department of Defense Information Assurance Certification and Accreditation Process (DIACAP), and Director of Central Intelligence Directive (DCID) models, for example, go as far as using these core concepts to develop, review, rate risk and monitor systems to apply the right management, technical and operational controls.

In comparing and contrasting privacy to security, security does not distinguish data from data that identifies an individual by default. Instead, security provides controls for risk management, including policies, procedures, guidelines and best practices that are typically aligned to technical, management or operational aspects. Although there are many types of security controls, there are actually only two forms of privacy controls:

- **Negative controls.** Enable privacy but constrain business (win/lose).
- **Positive controls.** Enable privacy and business practices (win/win). These minimize or eliminate threats and vulnerabilities and take advantage of opportunities to leverage data for the realization of business objectives.

It may be challenging for the privacy professional to fully understand the concept of security (protecting data) without protecting the identity or privacy rights of individual. The privacy professional should also be aware that IT security may always have privileged control of data and systems, considered a natural occurrence where individuals submit to security authority. In contrast, privacy operates within the boundaries of security. Thus, security does not always need privacy, but privacy always needs security.

> *"Security and privacy are not opposite ends of a seesaw; you don't have to accept less of one to get more of the other ... There is no security without privacy. And liberty requires both security and privacy. The famous quote attributed to Benjamin Franklin reads: 'Those who would give up essential liberty to purchase a little temporary safety, deserve neither liberty nor safety.'"* —Bruce Schneier[19]

Information security presented in a generic fashion addresses information security concerns using best practices from both the public and privacy sectors to include:
Three high-level security roles:

- **Executive.** Typically the chief information officer, Information security officer or other organization compliance officer
- **Functional.** Encompasses many operational responsibilities of security to include: security engineer, security operations and maintenance engineers, security professionals, and digital forensics professionals
- **Corollary.** These people support the security function to include: physical security, privacy professional, supply chain, and others

Fourteen generic information security practice competency areas created by the US-CERT IT Security Essential Body of Knowledge (EBK) include:[20]

- **Data Security.** Refers to application of the principles, policies and procedures necessary to ensure the confidentiality, integrity, availability and privacy of data in all forms of media (electronic and hardcopy). Key terms and concepts found in this competency include:

- Access control
- Aggregation
- Antivirus software
- Authentication
- Authorization
- Data classification
- Decryption
- Digital signatures
- Discretionary access control
- Electronic commerce
- Encryption
- Firewall configuration
- Identity data and access management
- Identity management
- Information classification
- Least privilege
- Mandatory access control
- Need-to-know
- Nonrepudiation
- Personally identifiable information
- Privacy
- Privilege levels
- Public key infrastructure
- Role-based access control
- Rule-based access control
- Secure data handling
- Security clearance
- Sensitive information
- Sensitivity determination
- Sensitivity of data
- Steganography
- System of record
- User privileges
- User provisioning

- **Digital Forensics.** Refers to the knowledge and understanding of digital investigation and analysis techniques used for acquiring, validating and analyzing electronic data to reconstruct events related to security incidents. Such activities require building a digital knowledge base. The investigative process is composed of four phases: prepare, acquire, analyze and report. Key terms and concepts found in this competency include:

- Anti-forensic techniques
- Bit-stream copy/image
- Chain of custody
- Cluster
- Computer forensics
- Copy/image
- Cyber laws/guidelines/policies
- Digital forensic systems
- Disk file system
- Duplicate image
- e-Discovery
- Evidence archival
- Forensic analysis
- Forensic labs
- Integrity of evidence
- Network forensics
- Network monitoring
- Persistent data
- Portable media forensics
- Security incident

- **Enterprise Continuity.** Refers to application of the principles, policies and procedures used to ensure that an enterprise continues to perform essential business functions after the occurrence of a wide range of potential catastrophic events. Key terms and concepts found in this competency include:

  - Alternate facility
  - Backup strategy
  - Business continuity plan
  - Business impact analysis
  - Business recovery plan
  - Crisis communication
  - Cyber incident response
  - Delegation of authority
  - Disaster recovery
  - Disruption
  - Essential functions
  - Information technology contingency plan
  - Interoperable communications
  - Mission assurance
  - Occupant emergency plan
  - Order of succession
  - Preparedness/readiness
  - Risk mitigation
  - Standard operating procedures
  - Test, training and exercise
  - Threat environment
  - Vital records and databases

- **Incident Management.** Refers to knowledge and understanding of the process to prepare and prevent, detect, contain, eradicate and recover, and the ability to apply lessons learned from incidents impacting the mission of an organization. Key terms and concepts found in this competency include:

  - Computer security
  - Escalation procedures
  - Incident handling
  - Incident records
  - Incident response
  - Information assurance posture
  - Information security policy
  - Information stakeholder
  - Information system
  - Intrusion
  - Measures
  - Personally identifiable information
  - Reconstitution of system
  - Risk
  - Risk assessment
  - Risk management
  - Security alerts
  - Security incident
  - System compromise
  - Threat motivation
  - Unauthorized access
  - Vulnerability

- **IT Security Training and Awareness.** Refers to the principles, practices and methods required to raise employee awareness about basic information security and train individuals with information security roles to increase their knowledge, skills and abilities. Key terms and concepts found in this competency include:

- Awareness
- Certification
- Computer-based training (CBT)
- Curriculum
- End user security training
- Instructional systems design (ISD)
- Instructor-led training (ILT)
- IT security awareness program

- IT security training program
- Learning management system (LMS)
- Learning objectives
- Needs assessment
- Role-based training
- Testing
- Training
- Web-based training (WBT)

- **IT Systems Operations and Maintenance.** Refers to the ongoing application of principles, policies and procedures to maintain, monitor, control and protect IT infrastructure and the information residing on it during the operations phase of an IT system or application in production. Individuals with this role perform a variety of data collection, analysis, reporting and briefing activities associated with security operations and maintenance to ensure that the organizational security policies are followed as intended. Key terms and concepts found in this competency include:

- Access control
- Antivirus software
- Backup
- Baseline
- Configuration management
- Insider threat
- Intrusion detection system
- Intrusion prevention system
- Patch management
- Penetration testing

- Security data analysis
- Security measures
- Security reporting
- System hardening
- System logs
- System monitoring
- Threat analysis
- Threat monitoring
- Vulnerability analysis

- **Network and Telecommunications Security.** Refers to application of the principles, policies and procedures involved in ensuring the security of basic network and telecommunications services and data and in maintaining the hardware layer on which it resides. Examples of these practices include perimeter defense strategies, defense-in-depth strategies, and data encryption techniques. Key terms and concepts found in this competency include:

- Access control
- Authentication
- Communications security (COMSEC)
- Configuration
- Cryptosecurity
- Defense-in-depth
- Emission security
- Encryption technologies (e.g., secure sockets layer [SSL], transport layer security [TLS])
- Firewall
- Hub
- Intrusion detection system
- Intrusion prevention systems
- Load balancers
- Network architecture
- Networking models and protocols
- (i.e., open systems interconnection (OSI) or TCP/IP)
- Network segmentation (e.g., virtual local area network [V-LAN], demilitarized zone [DMZ])
- Penetration testing
- Port
- Router
- Security trust
- Switch
- Telecommunications technology (e.g., private branch exchange [PBX] and voice over Internet protocol [VoIP])
- Transmission security
- Virtual private network (VPN)
- Vulnerability
- Web services security
- Wired and wireless networks

- **Personnel Security.** Refers to methods and controls used to ensure that an organization's selection and application of human resources (both employee and contractor) are controlled to promote security. Personnel security controls are used to prevent and detect employee-caused security breaches, such as theft, fraud, misuse of information and noncompliance. These controls include organization/functional design elements, such as separation of duties, job rotation and classification. Key terms and concepts found in this competency include:

- Background checks/background investigation
- Confidentiality
- Digital identity
- Human resources
- Insider threat
- Job rotation
- Nondisclosure agreement
- Position sensitivity
- Security breach
- Security clearance
- Separation of duties
- Social engineering
- Special background investigation (SBI)
- Suitability determination

- **Physical and Environmental Security.** Refers to methods and controls used to proactively protect an organization from natural or manmade threats to physical facilities and buildings, as well as to the physical locations where IT equipment is located or work is performed (e.g., computer rooms, work locations). Physical and environmental security protects an organization's personnel, electronic equipment and data/information. Key terms and concepts found in this competency include:

  - Access cards
  - Access control
  - Alarm
  - Asset disposal
  - Biometrics
  - Defense-in-depth
  - Environmental threat
  - Identification and authentication

  - Inventory
  - Manmade threat
  - Natural threat
  - Perimeter defense
  - Risk management
  - Threat and vulnerability
  - Assessment
  - Video surveillance

- **Procurement.** Refers to the application of principles, policies and procedures required to plan, apply and evaluate the purchase of IT products or services—including "risk-based" pre-solicitation, solicitation, source selection, award, monitoring, disposal and other post-award activities. Procurement activities may consist of the development of procurement and contract administration documents that include, but are not limited to, procurement plans, estimates, requests for information, requests for quotes, requests for proposals, statements of work, contracts, cost-benefit analyses, evaluation factors for award, source selection plans, incentive plans, service level agreements (SLA), justifications required by policies or procedures and contract administration plans. Key terms and concepts found in this competency include:

  - Acceptable risk
  - Acquisition
  - Acquisition life cycle
  - Business impact analysis
  - Contract
  - Cost-benefit analysis
  - Disposal
  - Prequalification
  - Regulatory compliance
  - Request for information

  - Request for proposal (RFP)
  - Risk analysis
  - Risk-based decision
  - Risk mitigation
  - Security requirements
  - Service level agreement (SLA)
  - Solicitation
  - Statement of objectives (SOO)
  - Statement of work (SOW)
  - Total cost of ownership (TCO)

- **Regulatory and Standards Compliance.** Refers to the application of the principles, policies and procedures that enable an enterprise to meet applicable information security laws, regulations, standards and policies to satisfy statutory requirements, perform industry-wide best practices and achieve information security program goals. Key terms and concepts found in this competency include:

  - Accountability
  - Assessment
  - Auditing
  - Certification
  - Compliance
  - Ethics
  - Evaluation
  - Governance
  - Laws
  - Policy
  - Privacy principles/fair information practices
  - Procedure
  - Regulations
  - Security program
  - Standards (e.g., ISO 27000 series, Federal Information Processing Standards [FIPS])
  - Validation
  - Verification

- **Security Risk Management.** Refers to the policies, processes, procedures and technologies used by an organization to create a balanced approach to identifying and assessing risks to information assets, personnel, facilities and equipment, and to manage mitigation strategies that achieve the security needed at an affordable cost. Key terms and concepts found in this competency include:

  - Acceptable risk
  - Annual loss expectancy
  - Annual rate of occurrence
  - Asset valuation
  - Benchmarking
  - Business impact analysis
  - Likelihood determination
  - Residual risk
  - Risk analysis
  - Risk level
  - Risk management
  - Risk mitigation
  - Risk treatment
  - Security
  - Security controls
  - Security measures
  - Single loss expectancy
  - Threat
  - Threat and vulnerability assessment
  - Threat modeling
  - Types of risk
  - Vulnerability

- **Strategic Security Management.** Refers to the principles, practices and methods involved in making managerial decisions and actions that determine the long-term performance of an organization. Strategic security management requires the practice of external business analyses, such as customer analyses, competitor analyses, market analyses and industry environmental analyses. It also requires the performance of internal business analyses that address financial performance, performance measurement, quality assurance, risk management and organizational capabilities/constraints. The goal of these analyses is to ensure that an organization's IT security principles, practices and system design are in line with its mission statement. Key terms and concepts found in this competency include:

  - Acquisition management
  - Budgeting process and financial management
  - Built-in security
  - Capital planning
  - Enterprise architecture
  - Enterprise security
  - Performance management
  - Strategic planning
  - Strategic resource and investment management

- **System and Application Security.** Refers to the principles, policies and procedures pertaining to integrating information security into an IT system or application during the system development life cycle (SDLC) prior to the operations and maintenance phase. This approach ensures that the operation of IT systems and software does not present undue risk to the enterprise and its information assets. Supporting activities include risk assessment; risk mitigation; security control selection; implementation and evaluation; and software security standards compliance. Key terms and concepts found in this competency include:

  - Accreditation
  - Application controls
  - Baseline security
  - Certification
  - Configuration management
  - Patch management
  - Process maturity
  - Risk assessment
  - Risk mitigation
  - Secure coding
  - Secure coding principles
  - Secure coding tools
  - Secure system design
  - Security change management
  - Security requirements analysis
  - Security specifications
  - Security testing and evaluation
  - Security vulnerability analysis
  - Software assurance
  - System development life cycle
  - System engineering
  - Technical security controls

The privacy professional should consult (early and often) the appropriate internal security resources to further understand and refine the use of these principles and concepts within the high-level strategy of the organization.

3. Privacy by Design

Privacy by Design (PbD) is discussed in both the *Assess* and *Protect* chapters of this book because the concept can be used in either or both based on the needs of the organization. The privacy professional should assess the organization's current and future objectives and goals in order to implement PbD appropriately.

The PbD framework dictates that privacy and data protection are embedded throughout the entire life cycle of technologies, from the early design stage through deployment, use and ultimate disposal or disposition. The foundational concept is that organizations need to build privacy directly into technology, systems and practices at the design phase, thereby ensuring the existence of privacy and appropriate controls from the outset. Originating in the mid-1990s and developed by the information and privacy commissioner of Ontario, the framework has gained recognition around the globe, including from the U.S. Federal Trade Commission and the European Commission.

Privacy by Design consists of seven foundational principles:

1. **Proactive, not Reactive; Preventative, not Remedial.** Privacy by Design anticipates and prevents privacy invasive events before they happen, rather than waiting for privacy risks to materialize.

2. **Privacy as the Default Setting.** No action is required by individuals to maintain their privacy; it is built into the system by default. This concept has been introduced in the European Commission's draft regulation to reform data protection.

3. **Privacy Embedded into Design.** Privacy is an essential component of the core functionality being designed and delivered. The FTC has adopted this principle in its proposed consumer privacy framework, calling for companies to promote consumer privacy throughout the organization and at every stage of product development.

4. **Full Functionality—Positive-Sum, not Zero-Sum.** Privacy by Design seeks to accommodate all legitimate interests and objectives, rather than making unnecessary trade-offs.

5. **End-to-End Security—Full Life Cycle Protection.** Strong security measures are essential to privacy, from start to finish of the life cycle of data. This is another principle the FTC has adopted in its proposed consumer privacy framework.

6. **Visibility and Transparency.** Component parts and operations remain visible and transparent, to both users and providers alike. Visibility and transparency are essential to establishing accountability and trust.

7. **Respect for User Privacy.** Above all, Privacy by Design requires keeping the interests of the individual uppermost by offering such measures as strong privacy defaults, appropriate notice, and empowering user-friendly options[21]

When followed, the principles of PbD ensure that an organization establishes a culture of privacy as realized through the privacy framework, mission statement, training and awareness. The organization, having implemented a tactical strategy to reduce privacy associated risks, may then be viewed favorably by its peer industry partners and consumers.

Figure 5.1: The Foundational Principles of Privacy by Design (after Cavoukian)

The PbD paradigm ensures that privacy and security controls are aligned with an organization's tolerance for risk and its compliance with regulations and commitment to building a sustainable privacy-minded culture. Notably, though, the paradigm is not a formal security/privacy engineering process (i.e., a system development life cycle (SDLC)). The qualities of the paradigm include:

Being Proactive. By default, privacy controls are part of the system engineering requirements. They are tested for effectiveness and monitored continuously. Privacy controls are embedded into systems and applications and are audited for regulatory compliance and evaluated when new threats to information systems are discovered.

Respect for Users. Privacy and security controls co-exist transparently to a user. They do not diminish the necessary authorizations to access data. The protection of organizational information assets is enabled without unnecessary trade-offs.

Privacy has historically been viewed as an impediment to innovation and progress, but that's so yesterday and so ineffective as a business model. Without user trust, technologies can't move forward.[22]

—*Ontario Information and Privacy Commissioner Ann Cavoukian, PhD, who has been encouraging organizations since the 1990s to embrace the concept of Privacy by Design.*[23]

4. Conduct Analysis and Assessments

To finish this chapter and to reduce confusion between *Assess* and *Protect*, we must now review conducting analyses and assessments. As with information security, analyses and assessments are essential elements of managing privacy-related risks. The privacy professional will determine where and when analyses and assessments should be completed as mandated by industry, organization policy or compliance to laws and regulations. Sometimes the need to perform such assessments arises from a data breach or other event and is a reactive risk management tool. Other times, the organization may need to assess privacy risks as a part of determining the feasibility of a business strategy or overall organizational goal—a more proactive approach. One tool used to determine whether a PIA should be conducted is called a privacy threshold analysis (PTA). There are several PTA models that can help an organization determine whether their system(s) requires a PIA to be performed.[24]

Analysis and assessments are the tools that facilitate implementation of PbD, allowing the privacy professional the mechanisms necessary to carry out the tasks of applying the PbD framework. Privacy Impact Assessments (PIAs), risk assessments and security assessments further assist in facilitating the *Protect* phase.

4.1 PIAs and Risk Assessment

The PIA itself is a methodology, or process, for assessing the privacy-related risks associated with business activities that involve processing of personal data: for example, projects, initiatives, systems, business processes, services, products, etc. As a form of risk assessment, the PIA assesses existing controls and also suggests or provides remedial actions or mitigations necessary to avoid or reduce/minimize those risks. To be an effective tool, the PIA should be accomplished early and upon changes to the methods in which data is handled (e.g., change in use of data or deviation from the original purpose for collection), types or extent of data handled (e.g., if sensitive data becomes part of the activity), or access (e.g., access by third parties, etc.). In some regions, PIAs are based on legal requirements (law/regulation), such as in the UK, Canada, etc. These risk assessments may also be performed pursuant to sector-specific regulations or requirements, in, for example, the healthcare context or banking/finance industries. Some regions, such as Australia, even call out the PIA as a fundamental component, noting that, "PIA information feeds into broader project risk management processes."[25]

Recent recommendations seen in the proposed European Data Protection Regulation includes use of a Data Protection Impact Assessment (DPIA) within the EU—similar to the PIA. This process, if implemented as recommended in the Proposed Regulation, would ensure "a conscious and systematic effort is made to assess privacy risks to individuals in the collection, use and disclosure of their personal data. DPIAs help identify privacy risks, foresee problems and bring forward solutions."[26]

The rationale for the recommendation is that "the introduction of DPIAs can contribute to improving transparency for individuals, as data controllers will be better informed about the risks connected to their data processing, and to the security of the processing of personal data, as data controllers and processors can better avoid privacy risks related to some types of processing and take mitigating measures for residual risks. This effect is further strengthened by application of the principles of *privacy by design and data minimization.*"[27]

Roger Clarke of the Australian IA Guide says the PIA is a "systematic process that identifies and evaluates, from the perspectives of all stakeholders, the potential effects on privacy of a project, initiative or proposed system or scheme, and includes a search for ways to avoid or mitigate negative privacy impacts."[28]

The Hong Kong Office of Privacy Commissioner for Personal Data defines PIA as "a systematic process that evaluates proposed initiatives or strategic options in terms of their impact upon privacy. To be effective a PIA needs to be an integral part of the project planning process rather than an afterthought. The purpose of this assessment is two-fold[:]

- To identify the potential effects that a project or proposal may have upon personal data privacy; e.g., the introduction of a multi-purpose smart card.

- Secondary, to examine how any detrimental effects upon privacy might be mitigated."[29]

Canada's PIA Guidelines define the PIA as "a process to determine the impacts of a proposal on individuals' privacy and ways to mitigate or avoid any adverse effects."[30]

The U.S. Office of Management and Budget (OMB) defines the PIA as "an analysis of how information is handled: (i) to ensure handling conforms to applicable legal, regulatory, and policy requirements regarding privacy, (ii) to determine the risks and effects of collecting, maintaining and disseminating information in identifiable form in an electronic information system, and (iii) to examine and evaluate protections and alternative processes for handling information to mitigate potential privacy risks."[31]

> *There are risks and costs to a program of action, but they are far less than the long-range risks and costs of comfortable inaction.*[32]
>
> —*John F. Kennedy*

Regardless of the geographical location or the requirements based in law, regulation or guideline, it can be said the PIA is a risk management tool used to identify and reduce the privacy/data protection risks to individuals and to organizations, aimed at ensuring a more holistic risk management strategy. Details of PIAs, how they are used, and formats, methodologies and processes around the assessments will vary depending on industry, private- or public-sector orientation, the geographical location or regional requirements and sensitivity or type of data. The privacy professional should identify the appropriate methodology and approaches, based on these various factors, and tailor the model to the specific needs of the organization.

5. Summary

The protect phase of the privacy operational life cycle embeds privacy principles into information security management practices within the organization to address, define, and establish privacy practices. One of the ways it achieves this is through the use of data life cycle management or data governance to manage the flow of information throughout this life cycle.

Endnotes

1 Rohan Massey, "What does it take to avoid costly data breach mistakes?" *The Privacy Advisor*, International Association of Privacy Professionals, Sept 1 2012, www.privacyassociation.org/publications/2012_09_01_what_does_it_take_to_avoid_costly_data_breach_mistakes.

2 Debra Logan, *What is Information Governance? And Why is it So Hard?* Gartner, January 11, 2010, http://blogs.gartner.com/debra_logan/2010/01/11/what-is-information-governance-and-why-is-it-so-hard/.

3 James E. Short, *Information Lifecycle Management Concepts, Practices, and Value,* 3 (University of California, San Diego August 2007).

4 George L. Paul & Robert F. Copple, *Data Life Cycle Management,* March 26, 2008. http://corporate.findlaw.com/law-library/data-life-cycle-management.html.

5 *Id.*

6 *Id.*

7 *Id.*

8 *Id.*

9 *Id.*

10 *Id.*

11 *Id.*

12 *Id.*

13 *Id.*

14 *Id.*

15 *Id.*

16 *Id.*

17 *Id.*

18 International Organization for Standards URL: http://standards.iso.org/ittf/licence.html.

19 Bruce Schneier, Wired Magazine, "What Our Top Spy Doesn't Get: Security and Privacy Aren't Opposites," January 24, 2008, www.wired.com/politics/security/commentary/securitymatters/2008/01/securitymatters_0124.

20 US-CERT, "IT Security Essential body of Knowledge (EBK)," www.us-cert.gov/ITSecurityEBK/.

21 *Privacy by Design; The 7 Foundational Principles*, www.iab.org/wp-content/IAB-uploads/2011/03/fred_carter.pdf.

22 Forbes, "Why 'Privacy by Design' Is the New Corporate Hotness," July 28, 2011, www.forbes.com/sites/kashmirhill/2011/07/28/why-privacy-by-design-is-the-new-corporate-hotness/.

23 http://privacybydesign.ca/about/.

24 The U.S. Department of Homeland Security provides an example of a privacy threshold analysis template, www.dhs.gov/xlibrary/assets/privacy/DHS_PTA_Template.pdf.

25 Office of the Privacy Commissioner, *Privacy Impact Assessment Guide*, 7 (2006), www.privacy.gov.au/materials/types/guidelines/view/6590.

26 European Commission, *Commission Staff Working Paper Impact Assessment*, 3 (2012) http://ec.europa.eu/justice/data-protection/document/review2012/sec_2012_72_en.pdf.

27 *Id.* at 68.

28 Roger Clarke, *An Evaluation of Privacy Impact Assessment Guidance Documents*, International Data Privacy Law 1, 2, 111–120, March 2011. www.rogerclarke.com/DV/PIAG-Eval.html.

29 Office of the Privacy Commissioner for Personal Data, Hong Kong, *Information Book*, 8.3. www.pcpd.org.hk/english/publications/eprivacy_9.html.

30 Treasury Board of Canada Secretariat, *Privacy Impact Assessment Guidelines: A Framework to Manage Privacy Risks*, Ottawa, Aug. 31, 2002. www.tbs-sct.gc.ca/pol/doc-eng.aspx?id=12451.

31 OMB Memorandum M-03-22, *OMB Guidance for Implementing the Privacy Provisions of the E-Government Act of 2002* (Sep. 26, 2003). www.whitehouse.gov/omb/memoranda_m03-22.

32 http://en.proverbia.net/citasautor.asp?autor=14002.

CHAPTER SIX

Sustain

"Sustain" is the third of four phases of the privacy operational life cycle that provides privacy management through the ***monitoring, auditing and communication*** aspects of the management framework. This chapter identifies gaps, verifies, documents and communicates the organization privacy management practices and principles for internal and external stakeholders.

1. Monitor

This section refers to ongoing monitoring of the organization to control, manage and report risk associated with privacy management practices. Monitoring throughout several functions in the organization, to include audit, risk and security practices, ensures "business as usual" for identification, mitigation and reporting of risk in variation or gaps in operations to meet regulatory, industry and business objectives.[1]

Monitoring should be continuous and based on the organization's risk goals through defined roles and responsibilities that may include privacy, audit, risk and security roles. Typical outcomes to practical and consistent monitoring programs include organizational:

- Compliance
- Awareness
- Transparency
- Creditability
- Validity

Monitoring privacy management over time and through consistent practices and reporting ensures privacy program open points are tracked, completed and locked down. Ensuring business as usual and closing identified gaps will assure privacy management and privacy protections. The privacy professional responsible for privacy and data protection should establish or identify the business-as-usual rhythms of the organization to understand how monitoring practices are used and maintained for privacy management and to validate that programs are being implemented in a manner consistent with the organization's privacy policies and standards.

1.1 Monitor Compliance with Established Privacy Policies

As discussed in Chapter 2, the privacy framework establishes the organizational privacy elements necessary to ensure compliance with established privacy policies, laws, regulations and industry practices. The privacy professional should review existing policies, processes and controls that make up the privacy program to identify gaps or opportunities for effective internal and external monitoring. Considerations as addressed in Chapter 2 include:

- **Organizational privacy office guidance.** If developed, offers the best starting point.

- **Review the definition of privacy to the organization.** As related to your program, organization, or industry. Use all available resources to determine a correct and appropriate definition of privacy for the organization.

- **Laws and regulations.** Provide the *mandatory government policy* and guidance based on the organizations geographical location and industry. Well-known examples in the United States include the Health Insurance Portability and Accountability Act (HIPAA), the Gramm-Leach-Bliley Act (GLBA) and the Privacy Act of 1974. Global laws include: the Australian Privacy Act 1988 and the European Union (EU) Data Protection Directive, which is implemented in national EU laws, such as the United Kingdom (UK) Data Protection Act 1998.

- **Technical controls.** Provide the means to automate monitoring by providing the *assurances* to achieve physical, data security and other goals.

- **External privacy organizations.** Provide industry guidance when none exists or provide guidance to strengthen current practices beyond legal or compliance factors. Some, such as the Center for Democracy and Technology, serve as a civil liberties group with expertise in law, technology and policy.[2]

- **Industry frameworks.** Provide *taxonomies* or *privacy categorization guidelines* that are non-law or regulation-based. Examples include the International Organization for Standardization (ISO), which defines itself as a non-governmental organization that has the ability to set standards that often become law, and the American Institute of CPAs and the Canadian Institute of Chartered Accountants (AICPA/CICA) Generally Accepted Privacy Principles (GAPP).[3]

- **Privacy-enhancing technologies (PETs).** Function beyond technical controls and could be considered the next level of technology innovation for privacy protection. They define privacy technology standards developed solely to be used for the transmission, storage and use of privacy data. Examples include Platform for Privacy Preferences (P3P)[4] and Enterprise Privacy Authorization Language 1.2 (EPAL).[5]

- **Information technology cutting edge or innovation solutions.** Involve the use of newer or unregulated technology, such as social networking and the Internet web cookie policy, for eGov 2.0.[6]
- **Education and awareness.** Provide methods to inform the employee of the important aspects of privacy and basic protections a non-privacy professional should know.

Technical capabilities should be considered a major factor to monitoring, as they reduce the effort and manpower necessary to gather, track, analyze and document the many transitions occurring daily on information systems. These automate many tasks that otherwise could take hours or days to complete and provide repetitive and consistent processes each and every time, bringing consistency and transparency to work methods.

Without a formal process to monitor and enforce privacy requirements, the organization cannot be reasonably assured that personal information is handled appropriately and aligned to the organization or compliance expectations or policy requirements. According to the GAPP, the monitoring and enforcement privacy principle is defined as "[t]he entity monitors compliance with its privacy policies and procedures and has procedures to address privacy related complaints and disputes."[7] Thus, the department that is responsible for monitoring compliance should also have authority to enforce compliance and work with stakeholders to ensure privacy and that all related findings, complaints or disputes are resolved quickly and correctly.

1.2 Monitor Regulatory and Legislative Changes

Depending on the size of the organization, industry or market affiliations, privacy, legal or other offices may have the roles and responsibilities for ensuring that the organization complies with all legislative, regulatory and market requirements. Given that laws, regulations and requirements are constantly changing and evolving, there is an ongoing need to monitor these changes; update organization policies and procedures in order to reflect these changes; and to maintain compliance within the privacy program. The organizational defined roles and responsibilities will determine who owns these tasks, when reviews must be completed and how those facts will be communicated to the organization.

An organization should have an established procedure to track and document all regulatory and legislative changes that are relevant to the industry. Based on the size of the organization or industry, there are several methods available for this, including internal and external methods. One way to stay abreast of changes is to subscribe to various alerts and updates, such as *Privacy Tracker*, the IAPP's legislative tracking service, along with the IAPP's free daily e-newsletter, *The Daily Dashboard*.[8] Another method includes using external vendors, which can also be found on the IAPP website.

The organization roles and responsibilities should define methods to disseminate identified regulatory and legislative changes throughout the organization and to the primary stakeholders. The speed and accuracy in delivery of this material maybe critical depending on the change; thus, a well-defined delivery process and communication plan should be established and updated frequently to protect the organization and communicate that change.

1.3 Compliance and Risk Monitoring

Privacy compliance and risk monitoring review the collection, use and retention of personal information throughout the organization information life cycle (also known as data life cycle plan). This ensures necessary polices and controls are in place for privacy management and compliance.

Organizations can establish what level of compliance and risk monitoring is needed for privacy management based upon the sensitivity of the information collected, compliance factors and the type of industry that the organization operates within. Monitoring should be done to ensure that the organization is actually doing what they say they are doing—and what they are supposed to be doing. Monitoring is essential to:

- Detect and correct violations
- Support enforcement actions
- Evaluate progress

The following list is representative of the approaches to compliance monitoring that can be used in an organization:

- Self-monitoring
- Audit management (internal and external)
- Security and systems management
- Risk management

1.4 Environment Monitoring

For a long time, organizations lacked technology that could help them carry out monitoring activities efficiently. Now, however, monitoring is becoming a more common business practice throughout industry. This can be seen throughout activities like information life cycle management through:

- Data life cycle protection[9] (DLP) that comprises the operational, technical and physical controls to protect the organizations data[10]

- Governance, risk management and compliance (GRC) initiatives is an umbrella term for the organization approach across the three areas to avoid conflicts, wasteful overlaps and gaps[11]
- Monitoring collaborative technologies, such as SharePoint, eRooms and network folders
- Monitoring all systems, applications and databases for use patterns

> *The acronym DLP, data loss prevention, is really just a subset of a broader issue better described as "data life cycle protection." The latter is the real issue.*

Some organizations have implemented monitoring policies and procedures that focus on external attacks using information security, such as the use of intrusion detection/prevention, firewalls and other technologies that are beyond privacy management but provide basic controls to protect the overall system and data privacy. These monitoring activities have focused almost exclusively on external threats, but today, internal monitoring is becoming as important as external monitoring and advanced risk management practices.

Organizations are thereby expanding monitoring focus to include threats posed by internal vulnerabilities. These threats or vulnerabilities include:

- Physical monitoring of building access, visitors and data center activity.
- Data access and authentication.
- Lack of awareness/lack of training, so that people do not know how they are to handle personal information. For example, they may send personal information unencrypted or don't properly protect the information.
- Insider threat as identified by Hanley: "A malicious insider is a current or former employee, contractor, or other business partner who has or had authorized access to an organization's network, system or data and intentionally exceeded or misused that access in a manner that negatively affected the confidentiality, integrity, or availability of the organization's information or information systems."[12] These include:
  - "Low-tech" attacks, such as modifying or stealing confidential or sensitive information for personal gain
  - Theft of trade secrets or customer information to be used for business advantage or to give to a foreign government or organization
  - Technically sophisticated crimes that sabotage the organization's data, systems or network[13]

Beyond the standard security monitoring practices, the organization should consider an array of different approaches for continuously monitoring key aspects of its privacy program, including:

- Ensure program goals for confidential protection of personal information are achieved
- Determine if policies, procedures and programs are being followed (protect the investment)
- Minimize consequences of privacy failures through early detection and remediation
- Provide feedback necessary for privacy program improvement
- Demonstrate to the workforce and the community at large the organizational commitment to privacy management

Monitoring can be done with systems, databases, representative activities, e-mail, desktop security, business area compliance requirements (e.g., conducting self-assessments, implementing monitoring controls), an exception process if a policy cannot be complied with, etc. Other areas that can and should be monitored include:

- Outsourcing of operations to vendors (e.g. subcontractors, third parties, etc.) who will be handling the organization's personal data. The vendors should be monitored as established in the contract agreement, in addition to vendors' protection procedures.
- Companies that outsource information to a cloud computing provider need procedures for monitoring that includes protections for:
    - Infrastructure as a service (IaaS)
    - Platform as a service (PaaS)
    - Software as a service (SaaS)
    - Storage as a service (STaaS)
    - Security as a service (SECaaS)

  Monitoring would include appropriate privacy and security requirements, as well as the cloud provider's performance, to assure compliance to contract specifications, laws and policies.
- Security monitoring for mobile devices, such as BlackBerries, iPhones and iPads to confirm that personal information contained within those devices is adequately protected.

Monitoring takes many forms, including:

- **Active scanning tools.** DLP network, storage, scans and privacy tools can be used to identify security and privacy risks to personal information. They can also be used to monitor for compliance with internal policies and procedures. For example, DLP scan results show that files containing personal information exist within public folders on the network and compliance issues exist with respect to the organization's policies, such as the minimum necessary access policy and storage and retention of personal information policy/procedures. They can also block e-mail or file transfers based on the data category and definitions.

- **Audit activities.** Include internal and external reviews of people, processes, technology, financial and many other aspects of the business functions. This aspect will be further reviewed in the Section 2 of this chapter, titled "Audit."

- **Breach monitoring, detection and notification.** Driven by the laws and regulations of countries, states or provinces, breach management practices are more important than ever before. Some of these best practices include:

  - Providing transparency to maintain good relationships with customers and regulators
  - Educating employees is critical to success
  - Knowing that old data is dangerous data—make sure you need to keep it
  - Avoiding collecting more data than needed
  - Being aware of social engineering tools that are being used creatively to gain access to personal information
  - Monitoring, enforcing and updating social media policies regularly without encroaching on employee rights
  - Avoiding access to trade secrets and other confidential information that puts organizations at risk
  - Encrypting is expected by customers and regulators.[14]

- **Complaints monitoring.** Although often part of country's privacy laws and good practices, all privacy programs, regardless of the industry or compliance factors, should contain compliance monitoring. A formal complaint-monitoring process will formally track, report, document and provide resolutions of customer, consumer, patient, employee, vendor and other complaints. This protects the organization legally and provides repeatable processes and tracking mechanisms to ensure transparency and accountability.

- **Data retention/records management strategies.** Data should be retained only for the length of time that there is a business need for it. Indefinite storage leads to indefinite waste and costs. Records management and data retention should meet legal and business needs for privacy, security and data archiving. Generic examples of improper data retention or records management policies may include:
  - Excessive collection
  - Incomplete information
  - Damaged data
  - Outdated information
  - Inadequate access controls
  - Excessive sharing
  - Incorrect processing
  - Inadequate use
  - Undue disclosure[15]

- **Dashboards.** Governance, risk and compliance (GRC) tools provide an automated means for organizations to identify, document and manage their existing risks and controls. GRC tools also provide a mechanism through which compliance audit and risk assessment issues/findings can be tracked, and corrective action plans can be managed accordingly.

- **Control-based monitoring.** Assessing the design and operational effectiveness of controls.

- **HR practices—Employee/visitor entrance and exit strategies.** Hiring and termination practices of the organization to control activity and monitor data and building access and use include security passes, system access, data access, visitor access to all organization resources and others.

- **Monitoring external conditions.** This approach monitors for risks that exist as a result of changes in the environment or changes to the industry.

- **Monitoring internal conditions.** This refers to monitoring as a result of internal changes within an organization, such as mergers, acquisitions and divestitures.

- **Regulation-based monitoring.** This approach monitors the organization for compliance to various regulations and requirements.

2. Audit

With the proliferation of the Internet and advancements in technology that have enabled data collection, use, disclosure, retention and destruction, implementing good audit practices ensures consistency, effectiveness and sustainment of organization privacy practices.[16] Audits are typically associated with the accounting or financial business functions of an organization, but in recent years have also become part of the broader business scope through risk management activities. Performed under different roles and business functions, audits perform "self-checks" and appraisals to detect irregularities by identifying risk and reducing potential threats to the organization. Based on the industry, regulatory compliance and other factors, audits are conducted by in-house (internal) functions, external third parties, government agencies, data privacy commissioners and others.

The Data Protection Act of 1998 defines audits as:

A systematic and independent examination to determine whether activities involving the processing of personal data are carried out in accordance with an organisation's data protection policies and procedures.[17]

Audit sustains the organization through monitoring and measuring privacy practices to laws, regulations, industry practices and other practices. The purpose of a privacy audit is to determine the degree to which systems, operations, processes and people comply with privacy policies and practices, answering the question, "Do the privacy operations do what they were designed to do, and are data privacy controls correctly managed?" The value of a privacy audit includes:

- Measure privacy effectiveness
- Demonstrate compliance
- Increase the level of data protection awareness
- Reveal gaps
- Provide a basis for privacy remediation and improvement plans[18]

Audits are an ongoing process of evaluating the effectiveness of controls throughout the organization's operations, systems and processes. They are concerned with improving compliance across the organization, rather than investigating violations or determining penalties. As such, audits can be used to identify risk through vulnerabilities and weaknesses (findings) and provide opportunities for improvements to strengthen the organization.

The role of the auditor based on the Data Protection Audit Manual includes:[19]

- Checking compliance status
- Assessing staff awareness

- Assessing organization privacy practices
- Identifying noncompliance and compliance
- Provide recommendations for corrective action

An audit may be conducted on a regularly scheduled basis (e.g., quarterly or bi-annually), ad hoc, or as requested to meet regulatory requirements, industry standards, or internal business objectives to measure your organization's ongoing privacy development and management against performance standards, laws or other directives. There may also be other reasons to perform audits, such as after a security or privacy incident has occurred or business function deterioration, based on several factors that include:

- Unclear, dated or changing polices
- Normal change management activities, such as system updates and maintenance
- User errors or accidents
- Hackers or security events
- Providing employees with insufficient training or use of the system
- Changes in the business, such as new categories of customers or operations
- Triggered events, such as VIP request, government request or media reports

Other nondeterioration factors that may drive the need for an audit include:
- Indications of an insider threat
- Staffing, cutbacks and changes to priorities
- New subcontractors or third parties
- Unusual changes, such as higher numbers of privacy breaches, complaints or incidents
- New portfolio or industry base

The scope of the privacy audit is important to determine the types of personnel who handle personal information, to include:
- Employees
- Contractors/subcontractors
- Third parties

Audit stakeholders, roles and responsibilities should be defined before the audit to determine ownership, need-to-know results of the findings and who is empowering the auditor to perform the tasks. The auditor must have full authority to perform the auditing duties; otherwise, the tasks and actions may be challenged and delay the work. These stakeholders include:

- Executive leadership, including the chief executive officer, chief information officer and chief information security officer
- Functional duties, such as privacy and/or security officers
- Office of the Data Protection Commissioner
- Government inspector general (IG)

The high-level five-phase audit approach includes the items shown in the figure below:[20]

Figure 6.1: Audit Life Cycle

These steps include:
- Audit Planning
    - Risk assessment
    - Schedule
    - Select auditor
    - Pre-audit questionnaire
    - Preparatory meeting/visit
    - Checklist

- Audit Preparation
  - Confirm schedule
  - Confirm and prepare checklists
  - Sampling criteria
  - Audit plan
- Conduct Audit
  - Meeting
  - Audit execution
- Reporting
  - Noncompliance records and categories (major/minor)
  - Audit report
  - Closing meeting
  - Distribution
- Follow-up
  - Confirm scope
  - Schedule
  - Methodology
  - Closure

2.1 Align Privacy Operations to an Internal and External Compliance Audit Program

Compliance audits take many forms and typically examine an organizations procedures, polices, systems, records, management practices, operational aspects and others factors to meet internal and external compliance that focus on:

- Compliance to legislation
- Compliance to data protection standards or industry guidelines
- Gaps and weaknesses
- Remedial action
- Improvements
- Positive and negative findings

The three types of audit categories include:

- **First party/internal audits.** The organization performs these with employees

- **Second-party audits.** Typically used in the EU but not the U.S.; include supplier audits for existing suppliers or subcontractors

- **Third-party/external audits.** Independent outside sources, such as data protection commissioner, government officials, or independent external assessment by subcontractors. These may align to ISO 19011 provisional standards through joint auditing of environmental management (ISO 14001) and quality management (ISO 9001) systems, or NIST SP 800-53 Rev 4, Appendix J.

Aligning the privacy program so that it functions and works well with both the internal and external compliance audits ensures efficient and effective privacy management that is communicated and updated. The privacy program must align with the internal compliance audit to prove the organization is self-regulating and to ensure the organization is doing what it claims.

2.1.1 First Party/Internal Audit

As was discussed in Chapter 4, an internal audit (IA) function may be enabled to perform auditing on the whole organization—all departments, functions and operations within the organization—or separate functions based on audit objectives and directives. Manpower, costs and limited resources will drive the need to determine the "best fit" and the more important business functions to review. Compliance factors will also play a role, as mandated by those regulations or directed by government offices/data protection standards.

As a management tool, internal audits are a form of self-evaluation in which the organization takes responsibility for monitoring and reviewing itself to assure continuous compliance, proactive privacy management and use of best practices throughout the organization. Internal auditors sustain the privacy program's "business as usual" by ensuring open points (e.g. actions, tasks and milestones) are tracked, completed and locked down. In a general sense, they may also evaluate the organization's risk management culture and identify privacy risk factors within systems, processes and procedures. Additional tasks include evaluating control design and implementation to ensure proper risk management; internal auditors test the operation of those controls to ensure the proper operation of those controls.

As discussed in the other sections and chapters and to repeat and reconfirm those topics, IA departments may report to an audit committee based on the organizational structure or may stand alone or within other offices, such as legal. Some, all or none may report to the board of directors, senior leadership, or some form of upper management. Based on the organization, the auditing staff may have a level of independence from the rest of the organization without disruption or pressure to present facts other than the truth. As such, the nature of IA maybe different from other groups, in that it may conduct internal risk assessments with more concern to represent the truth, rather than meeting management direction or management tailoring of audit results.

Audit programs evaluate a variety of systems, operations and procedures within the organization. An internal auditor may develop an audit work plan that will:

- Identify the areas to be audited
- Notify those offices of the plans
- Perform the meetings and reviews
- Provide all communications
- Draft reports and presentations
- Lead all management communications
- Close all audit matters
- Formalize reports and final meetings
- Perform follow-ups

The organization will need to decide on the types and frequency of audits, which may be driven by many sources, such as multinational or local laws, industry best practices or board of director guidance. Each organization is different; thus, each will have many factors that impact this decision.

2.1.2 Second-Party Audit

Second-party audits are typically used in the EU but not the U.S. As stated in the Data Protection Audit Manual, "They are commonly known as Supplier Audits because they are used where an organisation has to assure itself of the ability of a potential or existing supplier or subcontractor to meet the requirements … there is a tendency for organisations to outsource more and more of their data processing activities. Therefore Supplier Audits are becoming increasingly important as part of the process for making the initial selection of a data processor, and then for monitoring their ongoing performance."[21]

2.1.3 Third-Party/External Audit

When deemed beneficial or necessary through regulatory compliance, an independent external assessment could be necessary through subcontract to a third party, such as auditing firms. There are times when regulators or other people or entities will seek assurances beyond those provided by an internal audit. An example includes an organization who reports its financials publicly; for example, the internal audit department may perform audits to evaluate the organization's compliance with the Statement on Auditing Standards No. 70 (SAS 70); Statement on Standards for Attestation Engagements (SSAE) No. 16, Reporting on Controls at a Service Organization; or even direction from the International Auditing and Assurance Standards Board (IAASB). Internal audit findings may support the claim that the organization is in compliance with these standards. However, an external auditor will verify and provide data to prove the organization is compliant with those results.

Advantages of using external auditors include:

- Identifying weaknesses of internal controls
- Lending credibility to internal audit program
- Providing a level of unbiased, expert recommendations

Disadvantages of using external auditors include:

- Cost/budget
- Time or schedule
- Learning curve about the organization
- Confidentiality

External audits may provide an extra measure of credibility to internal audits. It's one thing for an organization to state that it has a strong privacy protection program. However, when an independent authority reinforces that self-evaluation with the findings from an impartial audit of that organization, there is increased confidence that the organization's practices are an accurate reflection of its claims.

2.1.4 Self-Certification Frameworks

Self-certification is a form of internal audit that does not exempt an organization from fulfilling obligations under applicable laws or regulations. Instead, self-certification provides the relevant facts, data, documentation and standards necessary to reflect consistent, standardized and valid privacy management that aligns to a particular privacy standard, guideline or policy. As an example, a well-known self-certification program is the U.S.-EU Safe Harbor Framework, which assures EU organizations that U.S.-based businesses provide "adequate" privacy protection, as defined by the EU Directive.

Failure to comply with the U.S.-EU Safe Harbor Framework requirements may remove all organization entitlements to benefit from the U.S.-EU Safe Harbor. Persistent "failure to comply" occurs when an organization refuses to comply with a final determination by any self-regulatory or government body or when such a body determines that an organization frequently fails to comply with the requirements to the point where its claim to comply is no longer credible.

2.2 Audit Compliance with Privacy Policies and Standards

"Business as usual" dictates departments and functions in the organization align to the organization's privacy requirements to protect data privacy as foundational business objectives and goals. Audits evaluate the organization to verify and prove that the organization is in compliance with the stated privacy policies and standards and to provide corrective action as necessary when gaps are found.

The audit measures how closely the organization's practices align with its legal obligations and stated practices and may rely on subjective information, such as employee interviews/questionnaires and complaints received, or objective standards, such as information system logs or training and awareness attendance and test scores. The results of the assessment or audit are documented for management sign-off and analyzed to develop recommendations for improvement and a remediation plan. Resolution of the issues and vulnerabilities noted are then monitored to ensure appropriate corrective action is taken on a timely basis. While assessments and audits may be conducted on a regular or scheduled basis, they may also arise ad hoc as the result of a privacy or security event or due to a request from an enforcement authority.

These are very basic, generic rules that auditors may use and the privacy professional can follow to ensure a complete and accurate privacy audit.

2.3 Audit Information Access, Modification and Disclosure

People in the organization handle personal information every day. There must be controls in place to protect that data and ways to track the data through its life cycle. As mentioned in Chapter 5, the organization should implement data life cycle management (DLM) practices, also known as information life cycle management (ILM), or data governance. This provides a policy-based approach to managing the flow of information through the life cycle from creation to deletion. It provides a holistic approach to the processes, roles, controls and measures necessary to organize and maintain data.

An auditor will want to know if the organization's DLM/ILM practices align with its privacy policies and requirements. Auditors may ask questions such as, "Who can access personal information? How is that information modified, or protected, while it is being used?"

An auditor will want answers to such questions as:

- Do information access, modification and disclosure accounting align with the organization's policies and requirements?

- Is there personal information that is known to be incorrect and needs to be modified?

- How is inaccurate information identified, and what procedures are in place to correct the information?

- What safeguards are in place to protect data from unauthorized changes? In other words, how is unauthorized access denied while allowing authorized access to the same data?

An audit will also look at processes in the organization to determine what controls exist to account for when, where and how this data is disclosed. This includes the way information is shared when outsourcing different functions to third parties. What controls protect this information?

Auditors looking at an organization's disclosure of data may want to know:

- Who has access to the data?

- Is data disclosed legitimately or illegitimately?
- Where does the data go?
- Are there clearly defined reporting methods for data disclosure?

2.4 Audit Findings and Communication with Stakeholders

After the organization has been audited, the auditors will prepare formal reports detailing the findings. If done correctly, the organization will gain valuable insight into the privacy operations, including:

- A formal record of what was audited and when
- Areas that comply and those that do not comply
- Details to support the findings
- Suggested corrective action, with possible target dates[22]

Noncompliant records discovered should be documented with sufficient detail to clearly identify facts and evidence to include:

- What
- Where
- When
- Why
- Who
- How

Specific report formats will vary, based on organization requirements, auditing methodologies, privacy framework and others.

The audit findings must be communicated to the affiliated stakeholders in the organization: all groups that are associated with that particular audit, like process owners, privacy office staff, data owners or other management. The stakeholders will then take into consideration such items as the following:

- Audit findings
- Risk level/degree of compliance
- Accountability for correction (action plan)
- Costs associated with the mitigation of the findings
- Approval of remediation process or justification for disapproval of proposed changes

Communication of the audit findings and reports is discussed next.

3. Communicate

Communication is one of the most effective tools an organization has for strengthening and sustaining the operational life cycle of its privacy program. Privacy information is dynamic and constantly changing. This means that for privacy policies and procedures to remain effective, organizations must continually communicate expectations and policy requirements to its representatives—including contractors and vendors—through training and awareness campaigns.

Improvements to the privacy program will also depend on the organization providing ongoing communication, guidance and awareness to its representatives regarding proper handling and safeguarding of all privacy data. All available means should be used to take the message to everyone who handles personal information on behalf of the organization. A good question to ask regularly is: How are we effectively communicating the expectations of our privacy program to the workforce—everyone who is using the data?

Each organization has need of a communications strategy for creating awareness of its privacy program and a specific, targeted training program for all employees. A goal of this communications strategy is to educate and make privacy program advocates of every representative of the organization. One of the best ways to accomplish this goal is by employing a variety of methods to communicate the message.

The privacy office is responsible for updating employees' knowledge when changes occur. Creating a strategic activities plan for the year is a good way to provide for regular updates. Some groups specifically build into their plan a designated amount of privacy communications to the workforce for the year so that they are continually refreshing people's knowledge. For example, "Every quarter we will have a targeted e-mail campaign that will go out to instruct employees on how to do x, y, z."

3.1 Create Awareness of Your Organization's Privacy Program Internally and Externally

An older meaning of the term *awareness* is to be vigilant or watchful. This fits well with the goal of awareness as it relates to communicating the various components of an organization's privacy program: creating a vigilant or watchful attitude toward the protection of privacy data. Everyone who handles privacy information needs to be alert to the constant need to protect data. No one is immune to the kinds of daily pressures and deadlines that can distract attention from the big picture. This reality underscores the need for organizations to put reminders in front of its workforce to keep attention focused on proper handling and safeguarding of privacy information.

Training and awareness—with the intention of changing bad behaviors and reinforcing good behaviors—is integral to the success of the privacy program. Many organizations have a learning and development group that manages activities related to employee training. This function enables policies and procedures to be translated into teachable content and can help contextualize privacy principles into tangible operations and processes. In smaller organizations, these responsibilities may fall upon the privacy function. Whatever the size of the organization you work for, the privacy team will always need to approve the training output that has been produced.

3.1.1 Internally

How does an organization build an awareness program internally? A good place to start is through inter-departmental cooperation to work toward the shared goal of privacy protection. For example, you may want to work with information security and tie your awareness program in with their awareness program. You may also look at including your organization's ethics and integrity department, as well as HR, to plan effective means for these departments to share their awareness programs and experience. Discuss ways that these groups can work together to get that message out to the workforce, creating an even greater awareness of your privacy program.

Another benefit of this approach to building an organization's awareness program could be that through the process of looking at the various awareness programs in place throughout the organization, you have opportunity to assess existing programs. This can reveal both strengths and weaknesses in individual programs, which itself is a positive result, contributing to an overall strengthening of all internal awareness programs.

3.1.2 Externally

Creating awareness of your privacy program externally has different requirements than those for building an internal awareness program. When promoting awareness externally, you don't have the same resources or controls in place that exist internally. External awareness is more directed toward building confidence through brand marketing. This occurs, for example, when your organization makes statements such as, "We respect your personal information, and we take X steps to make sure that your information is secure with us."

External awareness is directed toward building consumer confidence in your brand by creating awareness of your corporation's commitment to security or to fulfill a legal requirement. Does your organization have a reputation for integrity when it comes to handling personal information? This is the arena in which you create external awareness for your privacy programs.

An example of creating external awareness is found in the growing cloud computing industry. Many corporations are now exclusively, or at least heavily, involved in providing infrastructure, platform and software services for individuals and businesses. The marketing of cloud services is built upon the consumers' perception of the ability of the host organization to protect their personal information. And much of that information is personal information that other organizations are transferring to an external site for storage. The most successful cloud-hosting organizations are those that inspire confidence in their ability to provide security for the personal data that consumers entrust to them.

3.2 Ensure Policy Flexibility in Order to Incorporate Legislative/Regulatory/Market Requirements

Any changes to privacy policies likewise create a need for communication and awareness among all employees. The privacy office or other designated party has responsibility for updating employees' awareness of any changes that have been made to the privacy program. An organization's privacy policies must use language that allows for any changes in legislative, regulatory or market requirements, changes in technology and so forth to be incorporated into those policies.

The policy language describing policy requirements should not be so specific that it would leave out certain groups or that the requirements wouldn't apply to certain functions or departments. The point here is that the policy has to be flexible enough to allow you to account for any changes and be able to communicate those changes to the employees.

Flexibility includes the idea that you have to tailor your program to meet your organization's specific requirements. Legislative, regulatory and market requirements are not the same for everyone. Each organization must learn what requirements apply to their programs and develop effective methods for staying alert for any changes to those requirements.

As an example, the U.S. Children's Online Privacy Protection Act, or COPPA, enacted over a decade ago, requires organizations to obtain parental consent before collecting any personal information about a child under the age of 13. Recent revisions expand the definition of "personal information" to include a child's location, along with any personal data collected through the use of cookies for the purposes of targeted advertising. It also covers facial recognition technology. Websites that collect a child's information would be required to ensure that they can protect it, hold onto it "for only as long as is reasonably necessary" and then delete the information safely.[23]

Awareness regarding these requirements includes being aware of any changes to legislative, regulatory or market requirements as they arise and being able to incorporate those changes into your program's policies and practices. You will also need effective means of making your workforce aware of these updates and any adjustments that might be required of them as a result of those changes.

Again, a part of ensuring policy flexibility includes knowing what local and national laws, regulations and market requirements apply in order to determine what you will need to incorporate into that awareness. The type of organization you are determines what requirements apply to you and what you will need to build into your awareness program.

3.3 Identify, Catalog and Maintain Documents Requiring Updates as Privacy Requirements Change

There are two primary types of documents that an organization needs to maintain for the purpose of communicating about privacy practices: policies and notices.

- A privacy policy is generally an internal document that is addressed to employees. Policies clearly state how personal information is going to be handled. These documents serve as a vehicle for training staff, providing assurance that all employees understand their responsibility for personal information protection. There may be a variety of policies that detail how the organization will handle certain kinds of personal information, depending upon the purpose for which the information was collected. These policies must be clearly communicated to employees, so that information is not inadvertently used for unauthorized purposes.

- A notice is generally an external communication of the privacy policies to the customers about how their personal data is being handled. Notices are particularly important, because this is one means used by your organization to ingrain organizational accountability externally. Typically, notices are posted on the organization website.

Every organization is held accountable for what it says it will do and will not do with personal information. The FCC can take action against any organization in the U.S. that engages in deceptive practices, such as saying that someone's personal information is going to be used one way and then actually using it for other purposes that were not explicitly stated. In the UK, data controllers must notify the ICO of their processing activities. It would be an offense to process information in ways not included in the notification. Spain, Germany and France (and most of the EU) have similar requirements. Attention to details when it comes to policies and notices, then, is an essential aspect of sustaining your privacy program.

An organization needs to have specific, clearly defined means to identify, catalog and maintain documents requiring updates as privacy requirements change. The privacy office or other responsible party (e.g., legal) should have some procedure for cataloging and tracking the documents that reference privacy policy requirements and guidelines. This should be done to ensure that if any policy changes occur, all materials and resources that reference the policies can be appropriately updated to reflect those changes.

When policies are updated as a result of changing privacy requirements, those updates must be effectively communicated to everyone in the organization who needs to be informed. There must be a way to track policy changes and to ensure that all employees understand the changes and are in compliance. This need for accountability regarding policy changes might be addressed, for instance, through organization training documents.

The ability to manage changes and to maintain the program's viability in the process of changing is central to the ongoing effort to sustain a privacy program. Reasons for updating and changing the privacy policies and requirements for the privacy program include:

- Identifying opportunities for continuous improvement
- The changing regulatory environment
- Responding to changes in the business environment
- The development of new products and services

3.4 Targeted Employee, Management and Contractor Training

An organization needs to identify who will be required to take privacy training (e.g., employees, contractors, other third parties). By default, the training should include anyone who handles (collects, stores, uses) personal information on behalf of the organization. An organization that is proactive in its training programs will be in a stronger position to sustain its privacy program than one that is not as rigorous in its approach to training. To put it in other terms, the benefits of achieving a sustainable privacy program more than justify the various costs associated with developing a strong, proactive training program within an organization.

Targeted training implies that there may be a variety of training programs, depending on the department within the organization, the type of information that is being handled, how that information is processed and who handles it, such as marketing or HR. Responsibility for the training may also vary according to the nature of the work and its location within the organization.

All call center agents, as well as a new hire who is working in a call center, would require training in handling personal information given over the telephone and how to protect and secure that information (e.g., clean desk procedures). This training might be done through the privacy office or HR or by the head of the call center department.

Information security might conduct an assessment and/or provide training for a vendor who is building a computer program, writing code, and so forth for your organization. A vendor who is performing an HR resource, such as talent acquisition for the organization, would most likely be trained by HR or the ethics and integrity department. The training and who handles it would depend on what the vendor is doing for you. Training content should always be approved by a privacy professional, usually part of the privacy team—unless HR has its own dedicated privacy manager.

Training programs dealing with privacy policies should be based on clear policies and standards and have ongoing mechanisms and processes to educate and guide employees in implementation. Everyone who handles personal information needs to be trained in privacy policies and how to deploy them within their area to ensure compliance with all policy requirements. This applies to employees, management, contractors and other entities with which your organization might share personal information.

"Operational privacy practices" (e.g., standard operating instructions) refers to training related to specific operations, functions and activities that involve handling personal information. Certain groups require training on how to handle personal information that is specific to their group (e.g., customer service calls, collecting patient information). This is known as "function-specific" or "targeted" training.

Examples of operational privacy practices or procedures include:

- Data collection, usage, retention and disposal
- The protection and handling of data
    - Encrypting electronic data while in transit (e.g., e-mail)
    - Security for stored physical data (locking it up)

- Access control—who has access to specific privacy information and how is access controlled?
- Reporting incidents
- Key contacts or points of contact
- Function-, process- and department-specific handling procedures (e.g., collecting personal information as part of the marketing process)

After deciding who will be required to take the privacy training, it is necessary to identify the delivery method for the training. Various delivery options are available, such as online web-based tools and classroom-based training. Choice of delivery method may depend on available resources, the nature of the training, adult learning theory considerations and the locations and schedules of the participants. The important consideration is to choose a training method that will best achieve the desired results.

Another aspect of any training program is the frequency of the training of individuals. Some programs will only require a single training session (e.g., training that is conducted for employees when they are first hired). Other programs may require refresher training schedules that are specific to the training needs (quarterly, yearly or when changes occur). Whoever is responsible for developing and implementing training programs must be aware of any changes that are made to existing policies and regulations when they occur. Privacy training content is based in large part on policy and organizational requirements. When policies change, the training content must be updated to reflect those changes.

The department or other party responsible for the privacy training should make certain that some form of monitoring is in place to track compliance with the training requirement and its completion. In other words, there must be some way to ensure that everyone who is required to take the training actually takes and completes the training. Someone needs to watch the list to check on compliance and to record the results of the training. You should consider consequential actions that might be taken when compliance is not achieved.

4. Summary

The sustain phase of the privacy operational life cycle provides privacy management through the monitoring, auditing and communication. Monitoring identifies any gaps in an organization's privacy program; auditing ensures consistency, effectiveness and sustainment of the organization's privacy practices; and communication creates awareness of the privacy program internally and externally, ensuring flexibility to respond to legislative and industry changes.

Endnotes

1 "Business as usual," interview November 15, 2012, Mr. Simon McDougall.

2 Center for Democracy and Technology, www.cdt.org.

3 American Institute of CPAs, Privacy Maturity Model, March 2011, www.aicpa.org/InterestAreas/ InformationTechnology/Resources/Privacy/DownloadableDocuments/10-229_AICPA_ CICA%20Privacy%20Maturity%20Model_FINALebook_revised0612.pdf.

4 Platform for Privacy Preferences (P3P), www.w3.org/p3p.

5 EPAL 1.2, IBM Research Report RZ 3485 (#93951) 03/03/2003, www.w3.org.

6 Center for Democracy & Technology, www.cdt.org.

7 American Institute of CPAs, Privacy Maturity Model, March 2011, www.aicpa.org/InterestAreas/ InformationTechnology/Resources/Privacy/DownloadableDocuments/10-229_AICPA_ CICA%20Privacy%20Maturity%20Model_FINALebook_revised0612.pdf.

8 *The Daily Dashboard*: IAPP website, www.privacyassociation.org.

9 DLP comprises the operational, technical, and physical controls to protect the organizations data.

10 http://blogs.gartner.com/neil_macdonald/2010/02/24/its-time-to-redefine-dlp-as-data-lifecycle-protection/.

11 OCEG, GRC Capability Model™, GRC Technology Solutions Guide v. 2.1, www.oceg.org.

12 Michael Hanley, Tyler Dean, Will Schroeder, Matt Houy, Randall F. Trzeciak and Joji Montelibano. *An Analysis of Technical Observations in Insider Theft of Intellectual Property Cases.* Carnegie Mellon. February 2011. PDF.

13 Dawn Cappelli, Andrew Moore, Randall Trzeciak and Timothy J. Shimeall. *Common Sense Guide to Prevention and Detection of Insider Threats*, 3rd Edition—Version 3.1. Software Engineering Institute, Carnegie Mellon University, 2009. PDF.

14 "Data Breach Response: A Year in Review": Posted by Theodore J. Kobus III on December 27, 2011. Data Privacy Monitor. BakerHostetler.

15 Ulrich Hahn, Ken Askelson and Robert Stiles. "Global Technology Audit Guide: Managing and Auditing Privacy Risks." Institute of Internal Auditors. June 2006, www.aicpa.org/InterestAreas/ InformationTechnology/Resources/Privacy/DownloadableDocuments/GTAG5PrivacyRisks.pdf (pg. 4).

16 Hahn, et al. *Global Technology Audit Guide* at 12-16.

17 UK Information Commissioner's Office, *Data Protection Audit Manual*, 4.3, June 2001, www. privacylaws.com/documents/external/data_protection_complete_audit_guide.pdf.

18 Bruce J. Bakis. "Mitre: How to conduct a privacy audit," June 6, 2007. Presentation for the 2007 New York State Cyber Security Conference, www.mitre.org/work/info_tech/privacy/pdf/ HowToConductPrivacyAudit.pdf.

19 UK Information Commissioner's Office, *Data Protection Audit Manual*, 4.3, June 2001, www. privacylaws.com/documents/external/data_protection_complete_audit_guide.pdf.

20 *Id*. at 3.2.

21 *Id*. at 1.5.

22 *Id*. at 3.25.

23 Somini Sengupta,"Update Urged on Children's Online Privacy" (*New York Times*, September 15, 2011), www.nytimes.com/2011/09/16/technology/ftc-proposes-updates-to-law-on-childrens-online-privacy.html?_r=0.

23 Charlene Li & Josh Bernoff, *Groundswell: Winning in a World Transformed by Social Technologies* (Forrester Research, Inc. 2008).

CHAPTER SEVEN

Respond

"Respond" is the fourth of four phases of the privacy operational life cycle. It includes the respond principles of *information requests, legal compliance, incident-response planning* and *incident handling.* The "respond" phase of the privacy operational life cycle aims to reduce organizational risk and bolster compliance to regulations.

Every corporation needs to be prepared to respond to its customers, partners, vendors, employees, regulators, shareholders or other legal entities. The requests can take a broad form, from simple questions over requests for data corrections to more in-depth legal disclosures about individuals. No matter the type of request, you need to be prepared to properly receive, assess and respond to them.

> *It is important to note that although several countries, such as Japan, South Korea, Germany, Spain and Norway, have breach notification laws, breach notification actions in the U.S. are numerous. In the EU, there are pending changes in the proposed Data Protection Regulation.*

1. Information Requests

Organizations may receive a variety of information requests, such as:

- Complaints, issues, concerns from individuals
- Requests for information; e.g., for a copy of the public register of applications (German Federal Data Protection Act)
- Corrections of inaccurate data
- Clarifications on privacy matters
- Subject access requests (UK Data Protection Act and similar international laws)

1.1 Handling Procedures

Designing effective processes and procedures to handle privacy questions and complaints can be more complicated than one might initially contemplate. Organizations must balance the need to create processes and a structure that centralizes control with the need to delegate responsibility. Further, some privacy incidents do not fit neatly into the privacy-incident reporting framework—nor can they necessarily be adequately managed exclusively through privacy-incident reporting mechanisms. Some privacy incidents are so serious in nature that they require the involvement of stakeholders who do not typically get involved with privacy incidents, such as marketing, product development, general counsel, the chief risk officer and even the chief executive officer.

In managing privacy questions that may arise, it makes sense to leverage the privacy governance structure that you have instituted at a geographic and functional level to serve as the first level of response for commonly asked questions respecting privacy and security. Training and communications should instruct employees to initially reach out with privacy questions to these individuals. If "first-tier" privacy resources do not have the answers or do not feel equipped to adequately respond to the issues presented, then the privacy team or the chief privacy officer should be consulted. These first-tier responders should be strongly supported by the privacy team and the chief privacy officer with information material, FAQs and direct personal interaction. The channels of communication for asking and answering questions should not be too strict or formal. As long as local privacy resources and the privacy team are communicating with one another to ensure consistency, coverage and timely responsiveness, there are benefits to not being too structured. It is preferable to encourage personnel to come forward with questions.

While it is important to educate and empower these other resources to assist in the management of privacy questions, it is also important that they understand the limits of the privacy advice that they can dispense. They should focus on answering questions on established processes and procedures in areas where they have received specific directions—or areas that are materially analogous to the foregoing. Over time, this body of privacy knowledge will expand for the individuals and the enterprise. However, when first-tier responders do not have the answers, they must promptly involve the privacy team. It is important for the privacy team to have insight into the types and quantities of inquiries so any corrections can be made, gaps filled and issues addressed.

Complaint handling requires more formality than just responding to questions and inquiries. There needs to be a centralized intake process by which complaints are routed to the privacy team as quickly as possible. An escalation process should also be developed to ensure the proper handling of sensitive issues, including the possible engagement of key executives if the situation warrants. These processes will need to be constructed to handle complaints from customers, employees, business partners and regulators. As well, it is important to create and document procedures that track the intake, the management, and the resolution of the complaint. Many regulations—from EU data protection regulations to U.S. HIPAA to those of Canada, Mexico or Australia—give data subjects the right to register a complaint with the processor of their data, so implementing a meaningful procedure to substantiate compliance with this requirement is imperative. Additionally, the privacy officer and the procedure should be nimble enough to recognize when additional stakeholders might be required to address a complaint, such as the head of marketing, human resources (HR), the chief ethics officer, the chief risk officer, the chief security officer, the general counsel or someone else.

> *Privacy complaints (expressions of dissatisfaction) and the exercise of privacy rights (such as access requests) can be difficult to differentiate between in practice. If your organization has different teams or procedures for responding to complaints versus the exercise of privacy rights, there must be integration and/or flexibility to easily transition a customer or employee communication between the teams.*

Occasionally, the reporting or the complaint process respecting data privacy may intersect with an ethics reporting and complaint process. An incident may involve the use or misuse of personal information that may also qualify as an ethics complaint. Imagine a situation where the supervisor of an employee in the accounting department is using the personal information of customers or employees to engage in identity theft. The subordinate may be afraid to lodge a complaint or make a report for fear of reprisal. When ethics and compliance training is delivered to the employee population, employees should be encouraged to report these types of situations through the privacy reporting channel— but to the extent that the complaint clearly involves disreputable behavior, reporting through a compliance hotline might also be appropriate. Two important points to note— first, those individuals who manage the compliance hotline must be trained to recognize a data privacy issue and to immediately connect with the chief privacy officer and their team (or other privacy executive owner) and compliance hotlines. These types of hotlines typically permit anonymous reporting and must also undertake additional compliance efforts to ensure that they meet the requirements of applicable data-protection laws.

1.2 Access

You should develop a process so that individuals internal to your organization and individuals or entities external to your organization may reach you easily. You should have multiple methods and formats available, such as:

- Dedicated phone numbers (both direct and toll-free)
- Dedicated and monitored e-mail address (or multiple addresses)
- Internet or Intranet contact forms on the organization's homepage
- Postal mail box for correspondence
- Physical address

These resource accounts should be utilized within your internal and external communication plans. This will help make it easier for people to contact your office. The resource accounts may also be included within your incident-response breach notification letters or communications.

> *You should develop a written procedure for responding to access requests. This procedure will ensure not only that adequate verification takes place before access to data is provided but also that your organization is consistent in its reasoning for providing or denying access.*

1.3 Redress

The definitions of redress from the Merriam-Webster dictionary: a) To set right: remedy; b) To remove the cause of a grievance or complaint.

Both definitions are at the heart of the intent behind offering redress to individuals contacting the privacy organization. The organization should strive to remove a grievance or to set the situation right by doing the right thing for the individual.

The form of redress that is offered to the complainant should be clearly defined in your complaint response process and documented for resolution.

1.4 Correction

Depending on your industry, it is quite possible that you may collect personal information from varying sources and that the information needs to be able to be updated or corrected. A simple example would be a customer list when the customer has recently moved; their new contact information needs to be updated. This type of correction seems quite simple, yet it is important that you establish clear channels for this type of correction to be communicated.

Another form of correction could be when someone's identifying tax number is incorrect and could have consequences for the individual(s) associated with the number. Again, there needs to be a clearly communicated and documented process to allow the individual(s) to correct the misrepresentation.

1.5 Data Integrity

Data integrity issues are often the result of either human failure or systemic error.

1.5.1 Human Failure

An example of human failure regarding data integrity might be when a customer service agent is entering data for a medical benefit claim and inadvertently submits the claim under a different person's name (John J. Smith instead of John M. Smith). These types of human failures occur frequently. A process to resolve and handle these types of data integrity issues must be created and implemented to successfully navigate the issue. A strong training and awareness program is also critical to educate employees on the importance of proper handling and accurate handling of personal information.

1.5.2 Systemic Error

An example of systemic error might be when a payroll system is processing year-end tax reports and the data fields from one system do not properly align with the data fields of the reporting system. If the data fields are off by even one count, the data will be incorrect for all the subsequent records. In a case like this, it is possible that wage information will be associated with the wrong person. The restoration for such types of failures can often cost companies large amounts in fines and resolution costs.

2. Legal Compliance

2.1 Preventing Harm

The fundamental principle that should govern a privacy incident is to allow an affected person the opportunity to protect themselves from identity theft or other harm. This harm may demonstrate itself not only through identity theft but also through financial loss, reputation damage or embarrassment. Though the likelihood of an identity theft or other harm occurring from a particular specific loss or exposure of personal information is nearly impossible to predict, the principle of preventing harm drives privacy legislation globally. The likelihood of harm from a particular incident is low because statistics support the unfortunate certainty that most citizens are at risk for identity theft from several different vectors in the natural course of living their lives—meaning several probable exposures of their personal information. As a side note, there is a growing trend for criminals to target minors for identity theft, which in many cases is not discovered until the young person attends university, takes out a loan or opens a credit card.

> *The primary focus when managing any privacy incident is always harm prevention and/or minimization.*

In the private sector, liability clauses in contracts with data processors are paramount. In the EU, the default is well established that the data controller retains legal liability for any harm associated with the collected data. This default responsibility is only slightly less clear in the United States. In the U.S. and some other jurisdictions, it is perfectly possible to make the processor liable for remediation costs of events caused by their negligence if it is clearly stated in contract.

In the public sector, even with the proper implementation and monitoring of privacy and security controls, it is impossible to prevent all risks associated with government operations. It is inevitable that federal or other government organizations will experience privacy incidents, either internally or with an organization supporting the public sector (contractor) that serves as a data processor. Though a contractor may feel badly about a breach of data under their responsibility, the public entity remains the data controller or data owner and is required to make any necessary notifications. In extraordinary circumstances or under contractual requirements, a contractor may make notification to an affected person. For reasons stated below, this is not the best practical choice when viewed through the lens of the affected individuals. Unless stated in the language of the contract, in the event of a breach, the contractor should not pay for credit protection or monitoring, data-breach analysis, fraud resolution services (including writing dispute letters or initiating fraud alerts and credit freezes to assist affected individuals to bring matters to resolution), identity theft insurance or necessary legal expenses affected individuals may incur to repair falsified or damaged credit records, histories or financial affairs.

> *It is best practice to have the notice of a breach issued to the affected individuals by the organization that these individuals are likely to recognize from a prior or current relationship.*

Companies that do business with the public sector should avoid allowing the contractual burden of making notifications to shift from the government agency to the contractor. We note that the government customer is the owner of the data and ultimately responsible, regardless of the contract language. In some instances it may be appropriate for a notice to come from a contractor that operates a system of records on the government's behalf. However, in cases when a contractor provides such notice, notification procedures should be contractually established before the contractor begins operating the system. More importantly, from affected individuals' perspective, the best practice is to have the notice issued by the organization those individuals are likely to recognize from a prior or current relationship. This is also a good practice for private sector incidents in any jurisdiction.

Contract language between a contractor and a government agency may require contractor payment of a set amount of liquidated damages per affected individual to cover customer expenses. Costs for credit monitoring and associated average costs per record range between $35 and $200 per affected individual.[1] Once agreed upon in the contract, the amount per affected individual does not vary. The contractor does not have any responsibility to ensure the customer uses the money for the stated or implied reasons for payment following a breach. Best practice is that the contractor should not put itself in the position of actually providing credit protection or any related services. The contractor shall agree to essentially pay a "fine" in the form of agreed-upon liquidated damages per affected person. A contractor may choose to voluntarily exceed the amount of the liquidated damages payment for customer relations purposes but is certainly not required if limitations are clearly written into the contract. Deviation from the contractual agreement may create a bad precedent between the contractor and the government at large. The best advice is to negotiate the contract on the front end with appropriate standard limitations of liability clauses. These clauses limit the contractor's financial liability to a certain maximum total dollar amount or an exclusive remedy for the actual direct customer damages, capped at the contract value for the services provided or some lesser amount. Organizations should evaluate the level of insurance they carry regarding these types of matters.

The U.S. federal government has policies and procedures that govern how agencies must handle a public sector breach situation. However, the government requirements are not as rigid as many U.S. state laws. In many cyber incidents, notifications and other breach-related services by the government agency may be unnecessary. Guidance by the federal government cautions against making notifications when a breach poses little or no risk of harm and could create unnecessary concern and confusion. Office of Management and Budget (OMB) Memorandum M-07-16, "Safeguarding Against and Responding to the Breach of Personally Identifiable Information" outlines the government's procedures for determining whether notification is required. First, the organization should assess the likely risk of harm caused by the breach and then assess the level of risk. OMB M-07-16 provides guidance on the five factors that should be considered:

1. The nature of the data elements breached

2. The number of individuals affected

3. The likelihood that the information is accessible and usable

4. The likelihood the breach may lead to harm

5. The organization's ability to mitigate the risk of harm[2]

Stated again, federal government guidance states that when a breach poses little or no risk of harm, notification could create unnecessary concern and confusion.

Notification of a data breach to individuals is not always desirable. Where there is no legal obligation to notify, consider whether notification will assist in preventing or limiting harm—or whether it could simply result in unnecessary distress.

In the U.S., state privacy breach laws are used in most breach matters in the private sector, regardless of jurisdiction, if citizens of a particular state are affected. The impacted jurisdiction of the affected persons is likely the domicile of the affected person, but there are exceptions. In today's world, this is especially problematic for any organization that has employees or personal information for persons who may reside in a variety of states. Reporting requirements to state attorneys general or other government agencies are also different and inconsistently enforced. A robust and capable privacy office can only properly manage a multijurisdictional incident through proper understanding of relevant state privacy law requirements and attention to details regarding each affected person.

2.2 Accountability

A comprehensive privacy management program includes the concept of accountability and provides an effective way for organizations to satisfy regulators and assure themselves that they are compliant. Such a program helps foster a culture of privacy throughout an organization. Privacy accountability in an organization may be demonstrated through implementing appropriate privacy controls, demonstrating effective compliance using these controls, and documenting risk mitigation. An organization may demonstrate accountability through validation by an external regulator, third-party or internal self-attestation audit activity.[3]

> *Developing a robust privacy risk management program—and ensuring that employees are aware of and understand their obligations under that program—will naturally foster a culture of privacy throughout your organization and allow you to demonstrate accountability when so called upon.*

Accountability during a cyber incident (also known as "security" or "information security" incident) is different than general demonstration of the maturity of an organization's privacy program. There appears to be a wide variance between the number of known and likely cyber incidents and the number of public disclosures. Accordingly, it may be said that many organizations are not held accountable for their actions during a cyber incident and make a conscience choice not to make the required notifications required by state privacy laws. Based upon the number of privacy enforcement actions and fines levied by state authorities, it appears that organizations are rarely held accountable for not taking proper actions during a cyber incident. Organizations may not make required notifications out of fear of reputational damage or significant financial risk in the form of lawsuits brought by affected individuals or third parties. In the U.S., though many organizations fail to comply with state privacy law requirements, very few are held accountable.

Reputational liability is difficult to quantify. However, what about the fear of tort liability in the form of a negligence lawsuit? Aside from contractual liability, there is a risk that a party may sue an organization in tort, alleging they provided negligent cyber security protection and, as a result, damage was suffered. Potential damages include identity theft, financial damages arising from misuse of a credit or debit card, or reputational harm and emotional distress arising from a release of financial, medical or other confidential or personal information. Though many privacy professionals and practitioners are not attorneys, a basic understanding of the current legal landscape of privacy liability is worth knowing. As discussed below, the risk of tort liability does not appear significant and, in any event, is likely mitigated to a significant degree by the organization's insurance coverage.

Generally, to establish tort liability, a third-party plaintiff must show that the organization owed to him or her duty of care. In the data processing context, such a duty of care may derive from a purported obligation to prevent unauthorized access to or use of the data or financial assets of those with whom the customer has business relationships that are in the possession of the organization. In the cyber security services context, such a duty of care may derive from a purported obligation to provide services that will detect or prevent unauthorized access to or use of the data or financial assets of those with whom the customer has business relationships that are in the possession of the organization. However, data processing services are a service provided to the customer. Any benefit to a customer of the service is incidental and outside the foundation of the duty of care. An organization's cyber security services are designed to provide customers with the ability to detect and mitigate cyber threats to their systems and networks on an enterprise-wide basis. For the most part, services are not designed to protect specific customer or third-party data that may reside on or use those systems or networks, although protection of that data is incidental to or an indirect result of the services. In that regard, an organization's cyber security services are roughly analogous to the services provided by an alarm organization that contracts with a merchant to provide fire or security protection. In cases when the alarm or the premise monitoring fails and customers, employees or tenants of the merchant are injured by a theft, a violent crime or a fire, the courts have consistently held that, absent fraud or misrepresentation, the alarm organization has no legal duty in tort for personal injury or property damage suffered by third parties in connection with the alarm or monitoring failure.

Even if a duty of care is found to exist, a plaintiff must show that an organization failed to meet an applicable standard of care in protecting the data as a data processor or in providing cyber security services. The standard of care will vary with the circumstances, whether derived from industry custom, usage or another source, but it is important to remain mindful that an organization's duty under negligence law is not perfection, only reasonableness. Thus, an organization's services need not be error-free, nor are they expected to detect or mitigate every conceivable threat; their services need only meet the standard of care of a reasonable data processor or cyber security vendor under the circumstances.

Another major stumbling block for a plaintiff is the requirement to show that the organization's services were the proximate cause of his or her damages. In the cyber context, there are generally multiple factors involved with and causing a system or network breach, which may make it problematic for a plaintiff to establish a causation link between the breach and any acts or omissions on the part of an organization in delivering services. Aside from an error or deficiency by an organization (that typically leads to the greatest fines in the EU), a breach will typically involve:

- A third-party hacker or cyber criminal who intentionally exploits vulnerabilities of the customer system
- Customer failure to properly operate, use or secure its system
- Lost or stolen computer equipment (e.g., laptops, external drives, etc.)
- Misconduct of customer employees

In the case of cyber security being provided for a customer, exploitation of a pre-existing customer system vulnerability not disclosed or reasonably apparent that may result in the breach or otherwise interfere with an organization's ability to perform is an additional cause for a breach or damage to data. Although the existence of intervening or superseding hacking activity resulting in a customer system or network breach is reasonably foreseeable in the context of providing cyber security services, courts will typically require a showing of some affirmative action on the organization's part that creates or facilitates the opportunity for the hacking activity.

Under the current frameworks regarding accountability, accountability to a regulator usually occurs following a significant event that is poorly handled. The investigation by regulators will be in the form of "who knew what and when"—and a demonstration that the organization takes privacy seriously. Major components of that demonstration are the existence of a privacy awareness program, dedicated privacy team, breach protocols, and appropriate command media-enforcing regulatory requirements.

2.3 Monitoring and Enforcement

An organization should monitor compliance with its privacy policies and procedures and ensure there are proper procedures to address not only cyber security incidents but privacy-related inquiries, complaints and disputes. Organizations should fully document compliance with relevant privacy policies. Individuals within the organization should be aware of how to contact the privacy office with inquiries, complaints and disputes. Posting a dedicated telephone number and e-mail address linked directly to a responsible privacy staff member is advised. A protocol for investigating a concern and the ability to document the concern and its resolution is also advised. Monitoring controls over personal information through evaluating compliance with privacy policies and procedures is a component of a broader requirement to comply with applicable laws, regulations and other contractual agreements. A comprehensive compliance program will provide sufficient documentation and timely remedial action plans, as well as possible disciplinary action. Analysis of such monitoring controls over personal information is a useful tool for management.

> *Over time, monitoring and reporting on privacy compliance allows your organization to identify systemic issues and prevent compliance gaps from becoming endemic.*

3. Incident Planning

3.1 Understanding Key Roles and Responsibilities

This section focuses on the core elements of incident-response planning, incident detection, incident handling and consumer notification. Additionally, heavy emphasis is placed on a U.S. perspective to responding to data breaches, since the United Sates has some of the world's most strict and financially consequential breach notification requirements. The section begins by identifying the roles and responsibilities your previously identified stakeholders may play during a breach.

3.1.1 Know Your Roster of Stakeholders

Effective incident response requires systematic, well-conceived planning *before* a breach occurs. An incident-response plan's success ultimately depends on how efficiently stakeholders and constituent teams execute assigned tasks as a crisis unfolds.

The potential size and scope of breach-related consequences can't be understated. At issue are current and future revenue streams, brand equity and marketplace reputation. Other risks resulting from bad publicity include "lost opportunity" costs, such as high churn and diminished rates of new customer acquisitions.

These high stakes demand the inclusion and expertise of stakeholders from a wide range of job functions and disciplines. As stated earlier, the most common locations of personal or sensitive information within an organization are:

- IT or IS
- Human resources
- Marketing
- CRM systems of customer care and sales departments
- Audit and compliance
- Shareholder management

Reasons for including stakeholders from these functions in incident-response planning are obvious. However, involvement of other senior leaders in formulating and executing a plan that minimizes a breach's financial and operational impact is also essential. Doing so will ultimately result in a stronger, more richly multidisciplinary plan that enables breached companies to effectively restore security, preserve the evidence and protect their brand.

Examples include:

- Legal and compliance (in-house and outside counsel)
- Business development
- Communications and public relations (PR)
- Union leadership
- Finance
- President, chief executive officer
- Board of directors

3.1.2 Information Security (IS)

3.1.2.1 Role in Incident-Response Planning

The technical expertise and authority IS team members bring to monitoring access, inventory, storage and destruction of data make them essential contributors in any incident-response plan.

Knowledge of enterprise-wide configurations, networking and protocols, and security measures give IS a broad enough perspective of the organization's electronic assets to help them identify vulnerabilities before criminals (a.k.a. "bad actors") exploit them. As part of the incident-response planning process, the IS group will provide guidance regarding the detection, isolation, removal and preservation of affected systems.

3.1.2.2 Role during a Data Breach

Given the incidence and potential severity of external attacks, it is almost certain that the IS group will be engaged to address data compromises. As head of the team, the executive in charge will focus the group's expertise on facilitating and supporting forensic investigations, including evidence preservation. Additionally, IS will likely be tasked with overseeing the deletion of embedded malware and hacker tools and correcting vulnerabilities that may have precipitated the breach. Larger companies may establish a computer emergency response team (CERT) to promptly address security issues.

However, while internal IT resources may have the experience and equipment to investigate incidents, it is often more advantageous to bring in outside experts to identify the cause and scope of the breach and the type and location of compromised data.

3.1.3 Legal

3.1.3.1 Role in Incident-Response Planning

When developing an incident-response plan, companies should always seek the advice of competent counsel experienced in the field of data-breach response. If it's uncertain whether legal departments possess the requisite knowledge to fully address breach- and compliance-related issues, an assessment, overseen by the senior legal stakeholder, should be undertaken.

Legal stakeholders are central to incident-response planning because they, more than any other executives, understand the legal precedents and requirements for handling data and reporting a breach. Their guidance helps companies limit the liability and economic consequences of a breach, including avoidance of litigation and fines. In addition, most data-breach legislation requires intensive legal knowledge to implement a proper procedure.

During incident-response planning, organization attorneys may negotiate any requirements that the organization wishes to impose upon its business partners. Conversely, the organization may also use attorneys to help determine what it is willing to do in the event data belonging to a client is compromised.

3.1.3.2 Role during a Data Breach

One of legal's primary roles after a breach is advising corporate privacy and executive teams on response notification requirements: in particular, who should be notified, how and when. Such groups typically include:

- Affected individuals
- The media
- Law enforcement
- Internal teams (e.g. public relations or corporate communications teams)
- Government agencies
- Card issuers and other third parties

Legal stakeholders may also recommend forensically sound evidence collection and preservation practices and engage (or prepare statements for) state attorneys general, the Federal Trade Commission and other regulators. Stakeholders' knowledge of laws and legal precedents helps teams more effectively direct and manage the numerous interrelated elements of incident investigation and response. In the European Union, there may be requirements that data controllers notify regulators. You may want to make sure this is a person involved with breach management.

Drafting and reviewing contracts is another vital area in which legal stakeholders should be involved. If data belongs to a client, they can interpret contractual notification requirements and reporting and remediation obligations. Should the organization become the target of post-breach litigation, the legal stakeholder may also guide or prepare the defense.

3.1.4 Human Resources (HR)

3.1.4.1 Role in Incident-Response Planning

Given the extensive amount of personal information that typical human resources departments have on hand, it is highly advisable to include HR team members when discussing incident-response planning. HR staff may also be included because of their unique perspective regarding employees or for notification of current or past employees.

During incident-response planning, the HR stakeholders will normally address topics such as employee data-handling, security awareness training and/or incident recognition and response.

3.1.4.2 Role during a Data Breach

In the aftermath of a breach, the HR stakeholder may serve as the organization's informational conduit, working closely with PR or corporate communications to inform and update employees about the incident. During the breach, employees may become concerned about the effects an event might have on their employment, organization stock or strategic business relationships. Therefore, HR might work with internal or external resources to address and allay such concerns.

If an incident affects employee records, the HR team might also help investigators determine the location, type and amount of compromised data. If the breach is traced to an organization employee, HR would be expected to collaborate with the individual's manager to document the individual's actions and determine the appropriate consequences.

3.1.5 Marketing

3.1.5.1 Role in Incident-Response Planning

The typical marketing department has spent years, even decades, gathering, slicing, dicing and warehousing vast amounts of customer data, much of it personal information, individually or in the aggregate (name, address, date of birth, social security number, driver's license number, etc.). Through segmentation and analysis of such data, they gain the necessary insight to be both the "voice of the brand" to external audiences and "voice of the customer" to engineering, research and development, and other internal teams.

However, being stewards of such a rich data storehouse also increases marketing's vulnerability to hacking and unintentional breaches. This exposure, combined with the team's access to campaign and customer relationship management (CRM) databases, more than qualify marketing decision makers for a role in incident-response planning.

3.1.5.2 Role during a Data Breach

Marketers are expert communicators, especially skilled at researching and crafting highly targeted, consumer-driven messaging. Marketing can work with management and PR teams to establish and maintain a positive, consistent message, during both the crisis and the post-breach notification.

Direct mail expertise may also prove beneficial in supporting the data-breach response. Depending on organization size, marketing may control the physical infrastructure to help launch and manage a high-volume e-mail or letter notification outreach. Gaining internal agreement on the post-breach allocation of marketing resources is an essential element in breach-response planning.

3.1.6 Business Development (BD)

3.1.6.1 Role in Incident-Response Planning

The business development stakeholder, often aided by a dedicated account support team, monitors and manages vital business relationships. Companies with a certain level of value or prestige receive regular, personalized attention aimed at building trust, nurturing loyalty and sustaining the bond over time.

Stakeholders in this position gain firsthand knowledge into handling and keeping the account, including corporate culture, organization strengths and weaknesses, decision makers' personalities and management styles. These insights can prove invaluable in incident-response planning, which is why BD stakeholders should have a seat at the table when the planning process begins.

3.1.6.2 Role during a Data Breach

In the hands of a skilled sales or BD executive, high-value relationships can flourish for many years. Because of their unique association with customers and the bond of trust built carefully over time, BD decision makers are often asked to notify key accounts when their data has been breached. Receiving unfavorable news from a trusted friend and partner may lessen the impact and mitigate any potential backlash, such as a loss of confidence or flight to a competitor.

After obtaining the facts from IT, legal, PR or other internal teams, the BD stakeholder should contact the account and carefully explain what happened. Accuracy and transparency are essential. The stakeholder should stick to the known facts and under no circumstances speculate about or downplay any aspect of the breach.

Whenever possible, updates or special instructions regarding the breach should be promptly delivered by the stakeholder in charge of the account. This will provide reassurances that someone with executive authority is proactively engaged in safeguarding the account's interests and security.

3.1.7 Communications and PR

3.1.7.1 Role in Incident-Response Planning

Public relations and communications stakeholders are usually senior, media-savvy professionals who are highly adept at media relations and crisis management. They serve as stewards of public image and reputation, overseeing the development of strategic and tactical programs aimed at informing and influencing audiences.

3.1.7.2 Role during a Data Breach

When a data breach occurs and response teams are thrust into the fray (depending on severity), PR and communications stakeholders quickly assume positions on the front lines, preparing for the response to potential media inquiries and coordinating internal and external status updates.

Among their chief roles is to oversee the preparation and dissemination of breach-related press releases, interviews, videos and social media content. As the crisis develops, they also work to ensure message accuracy and consistency and to minimize leaks of false or inaccurate information.

During and after a breach, PR and communications teams closely monitor online and offline coverage, analyzing what's being said and to what degree negative publicity is shaping public opinion. Resulting analysis and recommendations are shared among key stakeholders and used to adapt or refine public relations messaging.

3.1.8 Union Leadership

3.1.8.1 Role in Incident-Response Planning

Though their numbers have declined since the 1980s, unionized workers still comprise a sizable percentage of the American workforce. According to the Bureau of Labor Statistics, the number of wage and salary workers belonging to unions stood at 14.8 million, or 11.8 percent, in 2011.[4] The AFL-CIO, the U.S.'s most prominent and well-known union, is actually a labor federation, consisting of more than 12 million members of 56 different unionized entities.[5]

As with all employees, data belonging to union workers is stored on organization servers and, like any data, is vulnerable to breach by accidental or unauthorized access. If their employer reports a data breach, union members will naturally look to stewards or other union leaders for information and guidance.

These individuals represent union interests and are authorized to act and speak on members' behalf—both to internal groups and to the media at large. For these reasons, any organization whose workers are unionized should consider including a senior union stakeholder in data-breach planning and response.

3.1.8.2 Role during a Data Breach

In preparation for a breach, union stakeholders should identify appropriate contacts within the organization and become familiar with its overall breach-response plan. Specifically, they should know the roles, responsibilities and sequence of events to be taken by other non-union stakeholders and response teams.

After a breach occurs, the primary roles for the union stakeholder are communication and coordination. Working with IT, HR or PR executives, the union steward may oversee the use of electronic communication channels, such as social media or union intranet or website, to provide members with timely updates and instructions. If member directories and databases are supplied ahead of time, marketing and call center teams can notify or update members directly through mail, e-mail or phone calls.

3.1.9 Finance
3.1.9.1 Role in Incident-Response Planning
In their response-planning capacity, the main role of finance stakeholders is to calculate and manage the bottom-line impact of breach containment and correction. Once the potential costs of responding to a breach are computed, it is up to finance to allocate the necessary reserves to fund resolution and recovery. The chief financial officer (CFO) should also champion more cost-effective measures that might help mitigate the risk of having a breach in the first place. To further aid in containing costs, finance executives or organizations procurement can help negotiate agreements with new or returning data-breach resolution providers.

3.1.9.2 Role during a Data Breach
During a data breach, finance stakeholders apply their knowledge of the organization's financial commitments, obligations and cash position to recommend budget parameters for responding to the event.

In companies where incident response is an unbudgeted expense, the finance team is often tasked with being both proactive and creative in securing the resources necessary to fund resolution and notification. This sum can range from several thousand to several million dollars.

Before or after a breach, finance executives may work with insurance carriers to negotiate insurance policy updates, including improvements to the general commercial liability (GCL) policy and the addition of "cyber" insurance coverage.

Cyber insurance is a relatively new form of protection that fills gaps typically not covered by the GCL plan. Organizations seeking first-party cyber insurance coverage have a surprisingly diverse range of choices, including protection against losses stemming from data destruction and theft, extortion and hacking, and revenue lost from network intrusion or interruption.

Notification expenses, such as printing, mailing, credit monitoring and call center support, may be included in a policy, along with third-party cyber liability coverage for vendors and partners. The CFO or other finance stakeholder can offer invaluable assistance in assessing the necessity and costs of updating insurance coverage.

3.1.10 President, CEO
3.1.10.1 Role in Incident-Response Planning
Executives lead; employees and stakeholders follow. In central business functions, the president/CEO's attitude and behavior set the tone for the entire organization. This is especially true with policies and practices surrounding data security.

Through actions taken (or not), and training funded (or not), employees can easily discern the value their leaders truly place on preventing breaches. Once data is compromised and the shortcomings of an organization's security practices become public, it is the top executive who will ultimately bear the blame. Though there are many strategic and financial reasons for including this individual in incident-response planning, this personal accountability may be the most compelling.

3.1.10.2 Role during a Data Breach

One of the first and arguably most critical steps taken by the top executive is promptly allocating the funds and manpower needed to resolve the breach. Having resources readily available helps teams quickly contain and manage the threat and lessen its overall impact.

In the period immediately after a breach, PR or communications teams will handle most of the media interaction. At some point, however, top executives could be called upon to publicly comment on the breach's cause or status. As with any organization attempting to manage a crisis, accuracy, authenticity and transparency are absolutely essential. Regular status updates from IT and legal, and coaching support from PR/ communications, can prepare the president/CEO for scrutiny from a potentially hostile media corps.

When addressing the public, executives would do well to follow messaging recommendations set forth by the communications team. This helps ensure message consistency and reduces the risks of speaking in error or going off topic.

The CEO, supported by the privacy team, might also be well advised to get in contact with the responsible data-protection authorities or regulators to discuss the incident and assure them that the breach is being handled from the top management.

With personal information exposed, peoples' lives and even livelihoods are at risk. Therefore, language and tone used to address the public should always be chosen with great care. The sensitivity with which an organization responds to a breach and executives' actions during the event will affect how quickly the organization's brand trust and customer relations are restored afterward.

3.1.11 Customer Care

3.1.11.1 Role in Incident-Response Planning

The head of the customer care operation must contend with issues such as high employee turnover and access to large amounts of potentially sensitive CRM data. These factors make customer care teams susceptible to various forms of attacks from intruders looking to access personal information.

Social engineering is an increasingly prevalent threat that can surface in a call center, as criminals call repeatedly to probe and test how security procedures are applied and how often they are enforced. In a recent survey of information technology professionals, more than 43 percent said they had been targeted by social engineering schemes in the past two years. And 60 percent reported that new employees are the most susceptible to attacks, according to a survey of 853 IT professionals.[6]

Aside from deploying the necessary technology as a first line of defense, employee training and awareness of these schemes can help to reduce the potential instances of an attack.

Conversely, when trained to recognize unusual employee or caller behaviors or to notice trends in certain types of calls, customer care teams can actually help deter criminal activity and prevent potential breaches. One central planning issue usually driven by the customer service executive is equipping and preparing call center staff, should they be enlisted for response support.

3.1.11.2 Role during a Data Breach

As part of their normal duties, customer care reps are trained to remain calm when confronted and to diffuse potentially volatile encounters before they escalate. Such training, along with experience working and delivering scripted messages in a pressure-filled environment, can enable deployment of these team members to effectively handle breach-related call traffic.

Using internal resources in this manner, however, could potentially degrade service quality for other incoming service calls. So the prospect of leveraging existing resources to minimize breach-response expenditures may only be attractive for certain organizations.

In companies where using in-house employees to answer breach-related calls is not an option, the executive of customer service should consider hiring experienced outsourcers to handle call overflow, or perhaps manage the entire initiative.

3.2 Integrating Incident Response into the Business Continuity Plan

To help operations run smoothly in a time of crisis, many companies depend on a business continuity plan (BCP). The plan is typically drafted and maintained by key stakeholders, spelling out departmental responsibilities and actions teams must take before, during and after an event. Situations covered in a BCP often include fire, flood, natural disasters (tornadoes and hurricanes), and terrorist attack.

To ensure proper execution of the BCP, all planning and response teams should know which stakeholder is responsible for overseeing the plan and who, within their specific job function, will lead them during an event. Knowledge of the plan, and preparation for executing it, can mean the difference between a successful response and a failed one, especially during the first 24 hours.

In terms of overall organizational impact, a serious or protracted data breach can rival big disasters. Like a fire, tornado or terrorist attack, a breach can strike unexpectedly at any time and leave in its wake damages of immeasurable cost and consequence. As with other calamitous events, cleaning up a "digital disaster" can take weeks, months or longer; in the aftermath, victims' lives may be changed forever.

In a 2011 survey of more than 400 IT executives in four major metropolitan areas, 85 percent said their companies had a business continuity plan in place.[7] One-fifth (19 percent) indicated that natural disasters, security and terrorist threats had made business continuity planning a much higher priority in recent years.

Considering a breach's potential repercussions and the benefits than can result from informed and thoughtful preparation, it's imperative that companies integrate breach-response planning into their broader business continuity plan.

3.2.1 Tabletop Exercises

Once breach preparedness is integrated into the BCP, incident-response training will likely be required. This training may take many forms, including workshops, seminars and online videos, but often includes "tabletop" exercises, a strategic mainstay of corporate trainers and business continuity planners.

A tabletop exercise is a structured readiness-testing activity that simulates an emergency situation (such as a data breach) in an informal, stress-free setting. Participants, usually key stakeholders, decision makers and their alternates, gather around a table to discuss roles, responsibilities and procedures in the context of an emergency scenario.

The focus is on training and familiarization with established policies and plans. Most exercises last between two and four hours and should be conducted at least semi-annually—more often if resources and personnel are available.

3.2.2 Updating the Plan

Soon after concluding the exercise, results should be summarized, recorded and distributed to all participants. Perhaps most importantly, fresh or actionable insights gained from the exercise should be added to the business continuity plan.

It's imperative to keep the BCP current. There is little strategic, practical or economic value to a plan that is painstakingly developed but seldom tested or improved. Those responsible should always ensure the plan includes the most up-to-date timeline, action steps, policies and procedures, and current emergency contact information (vital but often overlooked) for all plan participants. All those involved should be notified of any changes or updates to the plan.

3.2.3 Budgeting for Training and Response

Breach-preparedness training, especially in a large organization, represents a significant investment. Creating an environment that ingrains data security into the corporate culture and prepares teams to respond effectively requires an organization-wide commitment backed by the resources to see it through.

In most cases, the long-term financial and operational benefits of teaching employees to prevent, detect, report and resolve data breaches far outweigh the costs. The strategic upside of investing in breach preparedness includes:

- Exposing critical gaps in applications, procedures and plans in a pre-incident phase
- Greater overall security for customers, partners and employees
- Reduced financial liability and regulatory exposure
- Lower breach-related costs, including legal counsel and consumer notification
- Preservation of brand reputation and integrity in the marketplace

Though organization leaders often agree about the value of breach awareness and training, there is rarely consensus about who should foot the bill. Many businesses utilize a shared-cost arrangement that equitably splits training costs among participating stakeholder groups, such as IT, finance and human resources. Negotiations between them can include everything from funding levels and oversight to allocation of unused funds.

However costs are divided, companies should ensure that adequate funding is available to support business continuity and breach-preparedness training. To facilitate the negotiation, parties should focus on quantifying benefits, ROI and savings, rather than the bottom-line expense to any individual group.

3.2.4 Breach-Response Best Practice

Allocating funds for breach response is just as important as training, perhaps even more so. Typical costs incurred in responding to a breach include threat isolation; forensic investigation; engaging legal counsel; PR communications and media outreach; reporting and notification (including printing, postage and call center); and many other resolution-related expenditures.

Without a breach-response budget in place, companies may be forced to redistribute funds from other critical projects or initiatives. Having to openly debate the merits and value of one department's initiatives over another's may lead to tension between groups and ultimately delay or detract from optimal breach response.

3.3 Incident Detection

3.3.1 Privacy Definitions

Before we delve into privacy-incident detection and the security obligations shared among organization's varied departments, some basic definitions are in order. Generally speaking, a privacy incident may be described as any potential or actual compromise of personal information in a form that facilitates intentional or unintentional access by unauthorized third parties.

> *"Incident" and "breach" are often used interchangeably and may refer to a suspected or a confirmed compromise of personal information.*

3.3.2 How Breaches Occur

A 2012 study from the Ponemon Institute of 584 IT professionals whose organizations had been recently breached revealed that insiders and third parties, not hackers, are most often the cause.[8] It is interesting to note, however, that some of the most infamous breaches have been done by hackers. Forty-four percent of respondents admitted to being unable to determine the breach's root cause, but for those that could, it was most often a negligent insider (34 percent). Other root causes of breach cited in the study include:

- Outsourcing data to a third party (19 percent)
- Malicious insider (16 percent)
- Systems glitch (11 percent)
- Cyber attack (7 percent)
- Failure to shred confidential documents (6 percent)

Employee error or negligence is one of the biggest causes of privacy breaches. Ongoing training and awareness-raising around information security policies and practices is therefore essential in reducing the risk of a privacy breach at your organization.

3.3.3 Encountering a Breach

From their first day at an organization, new employees should be taught and encouraged to assume a "privacy first" mindset. When they observe that leaders and fellow associates are genuinely committed to data security and privacy protection, new hires are more likely to respect and comply with established reporting and data-handling policies.

Initial security indoctrination and training should also teach employees to recognize vulnerabilities and to capture (and report) basic information when encountering a potential or actual breach. Employees must understand when and how to report suspicious incidents to their supervisor, who, in turn, should know how to properly escalate the incident to internal authorities, such as the privacy office.

3.3.4 Reporting Worksheets

To emphasize employees' personal responsibilities when encountering a breach, policies and procedures should be a regular component of security training and refreshers. The following provides a foundation for developing your own incident-reporting or privacy training worksheets. These are merely suggestions and not intended to be a comprehensive list. All breach planning and preparedness resources should be reviewed and approved by internal or external legal counsel or by an expert privacy team.

SAMPLE WORKSHEET

Facts as they are known

- *Name and contact information of person discovering the incident*
- *Date and time the incident was discovered or brought to your attention*
- *Incident date, time and location*
- *Type of data suspected to be involved*
  - *Internal organization or employee data*
  - *Client or customer data*
  - *Third-party partner or vendor data*

Employee's description of what occurred

- *Briefly describe how you first discovered the incident or breach.*
- *Does the incident involve paper records, electronic information or both?*
- *What type of records or media do you believe were involved?*
  - *Paper: letter, office correspondence, corporate document, fax or copies thereof (copy machine)*
  - *Electronic: data file or record, e-mail, device (laptop, desktop or pad-style computer, hard drives in other electronic equipment; e.g., copy machines)*
  - *Media: external hard drive, flash/thumb drive, USB key*
  - *Do you know if the device or information was password-protected?*
  - *Do you know if the device or information was encrypted?*
- *Do you believe personally identifiable information like Social Security numbers, account information, user names or passwords were exposed?*
- *Can you estimate how many records were involved?*
- *To the best of your knowledge, has the incident been contained? (That is, has the data leak or loss stopped or is there still potential for additional data to be lost?)*

3.3.5 Notification Requirements and Guidelines

Escalation refers to the internal process of employees alerting supervisors about a security-related incident, who in turn reports the details to a pre-defined list of experts—typically the privacy office, which will then engage IT, IS, facilities or HR. Notification is the process of informing affected individuals that their personal data has been breached.

During the management of a privacy incident, it is imperative that all internal communications are "locked down" so that inaccurate or incomplete details regarding the incident are not sent around your organization. The incident-response team should be responsible for all internal communications regarding the incident; these communications should only be cascaded to staff on a need-to-know basis.

It's important to remember that not all breaches require notification. There are various types of notification requirements to regulators and affected individuals. If data was encrypted or an unauthorized individual accidentally accessed but didn't misuse the data, potential harm and risk can be minimal and companies **may not** need to notify (based on applicable laws). It is important to note that notification may be required even without harm to an individual. Assuming notification is required; businesses in the United Sates generally have 60 days to notify affected individuals. This may not be true in other countries, where newly developing regulations may have different notification requirements. The draft of the EU Data Protection Regulation in Article 31 only allows 24 hours for a notice to the data-protection authorities.[9] Wherever the affected individual resides, the countdown starts the moment a breach is discovered. Depending on a wide range of statutes, regulations and circumstances, the notification window may be even smaller. Certain state laws and federal regulations shrink the timeline to 45, 30 or even 5 days, so once a breach is confirmed, time is of the essence. Organization privacy professionals and those charged with incident-response planning and notification should be intimately familiar with the prevailing notification requirements and guidelines.

Incident-response teams should always confirm requirements with legal counsel experienced in data privacy litigation prior to initiating or forgoing any notification campaign.

Because of the potential consequences to the organization and to those whose data has been exposed, organizations must quickly initiate the notification process. This includes verifying addresses; writing, printing and mailing notification letters; setting up a call center and arranging support services for affected individuals, such as identity theft protection.

In the U.S., some states mandate that notification letters contain specific verbiage or content, such as toll-free numbers and addresses for the three major credit bureaus, the Federal Trade Commission (FTC) and a state's attorney general. Multiple state laws may apply to one breach, and notification may be delayed if law enforcement believes it would interfere with an ongoing investigation.

The notification deadline weighs heavily, in addition to the public scrutiny and already stressful ordeal of a data breach. Mishandling notifications can lead to severe consequences, including fines and other unbudgeted expenses. For extra support, some companies enlist the services of third-party breach-resolution provider to assist with notification, call handling and credit-monitoring offers. Lining up providers in advance can reduce response times and related costs.

3.4 Security Is a Shared Responsibility

Within any organization, data is viewed and handled by any number of individuals and groups and is often stored in several disparate locations—even across multiple states or continents. The potential for compromising sensitive data exists throughout every business of every size in every industry.

Regardless of organization size, however, all employees have a vested interest in being vigilant about safeguarding data. The cost of recovering from a single breach could potentially cripple an organization or business unit and render it unable to operate or fully employ its workforce. Therefore, teamwork, characterized by regular, open sharing of insights and information, is essential in detecting potential vulnerabilities that can lead to an incident or breach.

For example, whenever IT conducts security training, instructors may keep logs to record who has attended and who has not. IT may then share this information with HR to help ensure that every employee receives the instruction required by organization policies.

> *The potential for compromising sensitive data exists throughout every business of every size in every industry.*

Another example of cooperation between departments is how IT and HR might work together following detection of a virus or other cyber security threat. Typically, IT would detect the intrusion and prepare very specific containment instructions for all employees. They could autonomously issue these instructions or work with HR or communications to assure distribution to the complete employee base via all available channels.

3.4.1 Physical Security

In many organizations, the level of technical integration between IT and facilities is so deep and so extensive that regular contact through established lines of communication is essential to maintaining security.

But as technology advances, the lines of responsibility can begin to blur. Computers and systems managed by IT, for example, directly control doors, electromechanical locks, remote cameras and other access-limiting security measures maintained by facilities staff. This close association points out the need for ongoing collaboration if the safety and integrity of physical and digital assets are to be maintained.

3.4.2 Human Resources

Hiring, transfers, promotions or other changes in employment status may require revisions to an individual's data access privileges. When such changes are needed, HR, IT and facilities should follow established policies for monitoring and managing data access.

Another occasion requiring group coordination is employee layoffs or terminations. These are unfortunate but not uncommon events that can affect thousands of individuals or just a handful. In either case, the resulting threat to data security can take many forms, for which HR and other teams must prepare.

Disgruntled or resentful employees, for example, may try to exact revenge for the dismissal by stealing or destroying sensitive information. Others may attempt to obtain organization secrets or intellectual property to sell to or gain favor with key competitors. Before employees are terminated, HR must inform IT and facilities so that physical and electronic access for those departing may be turned off immediately after, or in some cases even simultaneous with, the announcement. Phones, equipment and other employee devices must also be wiped of login and password credentials.

Every organization must ensure that it has a procedure for retrieving portable storage devices or media from departing employees.

3.4.3 Third Parties

Sensitive data is seldom handled or processed in a single location. In today's global economy, huge volumes of personal information for which companies are directly responsible reside in systems and facilities managed by outside vendors, partners and contractors. These groups should always be accounted for in incident detection and planning.

To protect themselves and their customers, companies must have provisions in place that hold all third parties accountable for their data-handling practices. One method of enforcing security and accountability is through binding contractual obligations and reporting requirements.

For example, companies should make standard a clause requiring third parties to notify them within a certain timeframe when servers, websites or other business-critical systems are taken offline. It goes without saying that companies should always require third parties to promptly communicate any breach of data, so that contingencies can be made to mitigate resulting threats.

Conversely, it's vital for companies who work with third parties to remember that such communication flows both ways. If the organization's network is hit with a virus or comes under a cyber attack or there are changes to call center procedures or employee data-handling policies, the organization has an obligation to notify its partners immediately.

3.5 Tools of Prevention

To those on the front lines, prevention and detection bear many similarities to defending an occupied fortress. They must protect sensitive information against treachery and attacks that could come at any time.

Often, these challenges come from inside—new, careless or inattentive employees. Other times, cyber criminals, determined and well-armed, attempt entry by brute force or clever deception. Regardless of how they originate, if the fortress is to remain secure, threats must be detected and eliminated before it's too late.

Today, there are numerous weapons in a security team's arsenal of prevention. Some techniques are familiar but still quite effective, while others are emerging and showing tremendous promise. Below is a list of a few of the techniques currently being deployed by many organizations. The successful privacy professional will be mindful of the need to understand these measures and their intended applications and to be purposeful about keeping up with them as security technology advances.

4. Incident Handling

4.1 Pre-Notification Process

Once breach investigators conclude that an actual compromise of sensitive information has occurred, the pre-notification process is triggered. Steps taken may vary depending on several factors, but the purpose is to confirm that the event does indeed constitute a "reportable" breach.

4.1.1 Forensic Firms and Legal Counsel

Professional forensic firms prepare themselves to deploy at a moment's notice. Once on the scene, investigators work closely with the organization's IT group to isolate compromised systems, contain the damage, preserve electronic evidence, establish a chain of custody and document any actions taken.

Depending on the type of evidence uncovered, the affected organization may need to confer with outside counsel regarding their legal obligations. Breach definition and applicable reporting requirements usually depend on a variety of state and federal laws and international regulations, as well as the compromised organization's industry. Healthcare, for example, is subject to a different set of regulations than non-healthcare businesses. With so many variables influencing the "notify/don't notify" decision, advice from an experienced breach or privacy attorney can prove invaluable in meeting legal obligations and mitigating unnecessary costs.

As the forensic and legal analysis concludes, the decision whether to notify affected parties must be made. If notification is indicated, the incident-response plan must be activated and "go-live" preparations quickly initiated. While the organization's focus shifts to executing the incident-response plan, it is also important to continue addressing the cause of the breach.

Whether through employee training, replacing equipment, installing new software, adding staff, creating a new oversight position or replacing the responsible vendor, some action must be taken, and quickly. The situation that led to the breach should not be allowed to continue unchecked, or the entire costly exercise may be repeated unnecessarily.

4.2 Elements of the Privacy-Incident Response Plan

Immediately following the decision to notify affected parties, tactical portions of the incident-response plan begin to unfold. Generally, most well-conceived plans will account for and/or include the following elements:

4.2.1 Key Stakeholders

An incident-response plan cannot be executed without the direct involvement of the key stakeholders responsible for its design and implementation, as previously addressed in this book. Ideally, this group of executives/managers will represent departments that have been (or may be) affected by the breach and the subsequent response and recovery effort.

4.2.2 Execution Timeline

The incident-response plan is incomplete without a timeline to guide the execution and administration of breach-resolution activities. Close coordination among internal and external stakeholders will help ensure that all plan elements are executed in the proper sequence.

4.2.3 Progress Reporting

Keeping the response team on track and interested parties informed will depend on the quality and frequency of progress status reports. For complex or large-scale events, reporting on the number of letters mailed, calls received, credit-monitoring enrollments, etc., plays a pivotal role in distilling the chaotic reporting flow into a clearer, more manageable stream. Different types of reports will likely be needed to be given to different stakeholders, based on the need to know.

4.2.4 Response Evaluation and Modifications

Incident response can be tested with a variety of scenarios. But even a well-written plan can falter when the theory behind it collides with realities on the ground. As teaching tools, real-life breaches are far superior to hypothetical scenarios, so lessons learned from all incidents must afterward be captured, recorded and incorporated into the plan.

4.3 Developing an Incident-Response Plan

4.3.1 Team Leader

The most important person in an incident-response plan is the team leader. This individual will have ultimate responsibility over the initiative's success and will most certainly be called upon to make difficult and far-reaching (perhaps even career-making or career-breaking) decisions. Given this magnitude of responsibility, the team leader should be carefully chosen and uniquely qualified for the challenge.

Ideally, the person will be a high-ranking and/or well-respected executive invested with the direct authority to make critical business decisions. The leader should possess in-depth knowledge of the organization and have the skills to remain composed and professional under pressure. A proven record of effective crisis management is ideal.

Once appointed, the team leader will begin executing tasks outlined in the incident-response plan. Initially, these will include contacting and activating response team members and their alternates and holding a kickoff meeting to present the team with the facts and circumstances as they are known. The team leader may also conduct daily meetings to gather and analyze status reports and provide guidance, as needed.

The team leader may also choose to provide senior executives with an overview of the event and of the team's expected course of action. Convening with individual stakeholders to discuss lawsuits, media inquiries, regulatory concerns and other pressing developments is another of the team leader's tasks.

During the breach, team leaders will also:

- Keep individual response-team members on track to meet their performance objectives and timelines
- Track budget adherence for all response activities
- Contact outside incident-response resources to confirm engagement and monitor performance
- Prepare a final analysis of the response effort and lead the post-event evaluation process

4.3.2 Response Team Members

The response team should include employees from all departments that are or may be involved with or informed about the incident. In the initial stages of response, it is better to over-communicate than to neglect departments that should have been involved. As a rule, the following stakeholders should *always* be integrated into the response team.

4.3.2.1 IT and IS

During a breach, the chief technology officer (CTO), or similar high-ranking executive, typically represents the technology and/or information security departments.

The CTO's role may include recommending outside forensic experts to help ascertain the incident's cause, size and scope. The CTO may also oversee evidence preservation, taking affected systems offline and correcting vulnerabilities that facilitated the incident.

To support other groups with their breach-response efforts, the technology team may also:

- Provide a secure transmission method for data files intended for the print vendor or incident call center
- Identify the location of potentially compromised data (test, development and production environments)
- Determine the number of records potentially affected and the types of personal information they contain
- Clean up mailing lists to help facilitate the printing process
- Sort through data to identify populations requiring special handling (minors, expatriates, deceased, etc.)
- Monitor systems for additional attacks
- Fix the gaps in the IT systems, if applicable

4.3.2.2 Legal

Whether through its general counsel, chief privacy officer (CPO) or chief compliance officer (CCO), an organization affected by a breach must seek competent legal counsel to ensure proper adherence to their legal obligations. Many times, outside attorneys are best positioned to advise on breach-related matters. In addition to confirming the need to contact victims, counsel may also deem it necessary for the organization to:

- Notify regulators and law enforcement
- Respond to media inquiries
- Alert credit card issuers and credit reporting agencies
- Negotiate contracts with breach-related providers
- Review existing contracts to clearly understand the organization's commitments to clients, as well the obligations of providers toward the organization
- Help manage breach investigation and evidence preservation
- Review all communications for possible legal liability

4.3.2.3 Human Resources (HR)

Whether breaches affect employees' data or not, the chief human resources officer (CHRO) or vice president of human resources must guide the HR team's response activities. Concerns over the organization's solvency or stock value can make it necessary to inform employees of the incident and steps being taken to resolve it. In addition, employees might be contacted in regards to the incident by affected persons, the media or other parties.

If employee data is compromised, the CHRO's role will become more prominent, including directing the HR team in identifying the cause and scope and overseeing communications between management and staff. If the breach is attributed to an employee, the HR group will take one or more of the following actions: provide training, make procedural changes, administer the appropriate corrective action, or terminate the individual. If criminal behavior is discovered, the legal department and/or law enforcement officials may become involved.

During and after a breach, the HR team may be called upon to perform a variety of other corrective or educational tasks, such as:

- Facilitating employee interviews with internal and external investigators
- Identifying individuals who are in need of training
- Holding daily meetings to summarize breach updates and create appropriate communications for employees
- Escalating concerns to the appropriate department heads

4.3.2.4 Finance

The chief financial officer (CFO) or the chief financial and operating officer (CFOO) will be responsible for guiding the organization's post-breach financial decisions. Since breaches tend to be unplanned, unbudgeted events, the CFO should work closely with senior management to allocate and acquire the funds necessary to fully recover from the event.

The CFO may help negotiate with outside providers to obtain favorable pricing and terms of service. The finance team may also collaborate with the legal group to create cost/benefit models that identify the most practical or economical approaches.

Tasks commonly undertaken by the finance team during a breach include:

- Setting aside and managing appropriate reserves to pay for rapidly mounting expenses
- Working with vendors to extend payment terms and secure potential discounts
- Promptly paying invoices for breach-related activities
- Meeting daily with the response team leader to track incident expenses
- Requesting ongoing reports from breach providers to manage and track call center, printing and credit-monitoring costs

4.3.2.5 Marketing and PR

The chief marketing officer (CMO) is the person best qualified to help mitigate brand/reputational damage that can follow a data breach. By collaborating with the public relations team or crisis management firm, the CMO can oversee content development for press releases, blog and website updates, and victim notification letters. Monitoring and responding to media coverage and arranging spokesperson interviews will also fall to members of the CMO's team.

Since the marketing department may already have the expertise and infrastructure in place to support large-scale mailings, the CMO could divert resources necessary to facilitate the notification process. In support of the effort, the team may also:

- Suggest direct marketing best practices to maximize notification letter open rates
- Perform address/database hygiene to improve breach notification delivery and response rates
- Analyze media coverage and report relevant developments to the response team
- Draft scripts for the incident-response call center
- Develop customer retention and win-back campaigns to minimize churn and encourage loyalty

4.3.2.6 Customer Care

In the aftermath of a breach, customer service can recommend ways of using internal sources to serve the needs of breach victims and identify an appropriate outsourced partner. This stakeholder is also likely to work with others to coordinate the release of breach-related communications with call center readiness and activities.

Given the customer service training and experience of most call center teams, using existing staffing and assets to address breach-related inquiries may be a viable time- and cost-saving option for some companies. If an outsourced provider is retained to answer incoming calls, the customer service executive can play a crucial role in determining acceptable service levels, reporting duties and necessary service-rep training.

4.3.2.7 Outside Resources

In addition to support of internal functional leaders, a successful response may depend heavily on the aid of outside specialists retained to manage notification, call center and breach-remediation activities. It is a best practice to negotiate agreements with experienced breach-response providers prior to having to respond to an incident.

4.3.2.8 Print Vendors

A reputable print provider, for example, can be invaluable in leveraging its equipment and assets to produce, stuff, mail and track large volumes of letters. The print vendor may also guide the breach-response team leader and appropriate support staff through the notification effort's many technical details. Important but less obvious support activities, such as gathering logos, sample signatures, letter copy and address files, must also be completed as production and delivery deadlines approach.

4.3.2.9 Call Center

Once notification letters are delivered, recipients will begin calling and e-mailing the organization to inquire about the event and its impact on their lives. In situations where projected call volume is large enough for call center outsourcing, it is crucial that the team leader fully understand the vendor's overall capabilities. As soon as possible, agreements should be reached and the timeline set for training and assigning agents, call-routing programming, message recording, service level agreements (SLAs) and call center reporting.

4.3.2.10 Remediation Providers

Depending on the nature of the information compromised, breached organizations may choose to engage remediation providers to reduce consumers' risk of fraud or identity theft. This may include a third-party credit-activity monitoring service. The service should be offered free to the consumer and include, at minimum: daily monitoring and alerts of activity from all three national credit bureaus; identity theft insurance and fraud resolution services. In some cases, supplemental services, such as Internet scanning (for compromised information), may also be deployed to help protect consumers.

4.4 Execution Timeline

No strategy is bulletproof, and no timeline perfect. But the crucial execution phase of the incident-response plan is particularly susceptible to setbacks if realistic, properly sequenced timelines are not observed.

Because of organizations' vastly differing cultural, political and regulatory considerations, it is usually not practical to prescribe a rigid, one-size-fits-all breach-event timeline. There is value, however, in including some or all of the following communication tactics when formulating a breach response.

4.4.1 Internal Announcements

Attempting to keep employees from learning of a data loss is neither prudent nor possible. On the contrary, transparency is paramount to maintaining integrity and credibility. When a breach occurs, all employees should receive properly worded communications about the event, along with specific guidelines and prohibitions about externally disseminating information. Internal breach announcements should be timed so as to not conflict with other organization initiatives. To minimize the chance of leaks, these announcements should also be delivered about the same time as external statements.

A breach may affect an organization's real or perceived financial viability, so the HR team should prepare to address a range of employee concerns. If an event has occurred but does not affect employees directly, these activities may help supplement the internal announcement process:

- Creation, approval and posting of employee-only FAQs
- Response training for HR personnel and call center staff
- Creation, approval and distribution of explanatory letter, e-mail or intranet communications.

4.4.2 External Announcements

The creation and release of external communications should be closely coordinated with the call center. In addition to notification letters and press releases, other external strategies and tactics may be deployed to announce and manage breach communications. Among the most important of these is engaging a professional crisis management or communications firm (if none are available internally) and designating a senior, media-trained executive as organization spokesperson.

Talking points should also be developed as quickly as possible, so the spokesperson may confidently address the media. For consistency, foundational message points can be used to create content for press releases, intranets, organization website and call center incident-handling FAQs. A dedicated toll-free number should be secured and routed to the correct call center to properly handle incoming calls.

Other considerations for preparing external announcements include:

- Call center FAQ review and training
- Staffing-level assessment to ensure adequate coverage
- Closely timing external and internal releases

4.4.3 Regulator Notifications

Legal counsel should provide guidance on which state, federal or international regulatory agencies require notification in the event of a data breach. In many instances in the U.S., it is appropriate to contact the state attorney general and, in some cases, the FTC. In the healthcare industry, Department of Health and Human Services may need to be notified as well. Notification to these agencies would be determined on a case-by-case basis, depending on the size and scope of the data breach; seek a legal professional with data-breach experience for guidance.

4.4.4 Letter Drops

Letters and e-mails are the most common forms of breach notification. As organizations decide to notify, the need to meet specific deadlines in accordance with applicable laws while working within the constraints of complex production and delivery processes can be unwieldy and difficult to reconcile.

Unlike outputting documents from a PC, industrial-level printing requires a great deal of preparation and quality control. Verifying mailing file completeness, format consistency, and age of mailing list data can add days to the production timeline. Moreover, changing content during production or delivering assets (logos, signatures, copy) after specified deadlines can unnecessarily delay notification and burn precious days in an already accelerated schedule.

Here are some time-proven methods for ensuring a more efficient process:

- If appropriate, establish a secure data-transfer channel
- Create letter copy and put it into Microsoft Word format (or other preferred format)
- Obtain any necessary content approvals from the compliance and/or legal team
- Send usable data files to the print shop, including a properly formatted logo and electronic signature
- Supply a return address for undeliverable mail
- Review final letter layout for a legible, aesthetically pleasing appearance

When planning letter drops, remember that a data breach may also involve criminal activity and, therefore, law enforcement personnel. If officials determine that the notification will impede their investigation or threaten national security, delays can be expected.

4.4.5 Call Center Launches

Call centers normally in place have the infrastructure, policies and procedures needed to seamlessly switch from providing general customer service to answering breach-related calls. For a switch to be successful, proper preparation for every call center component is required. Adequately staffing the incident-response team is one particularly critical consideration.

To increase headcount, temp agencies or outsourcers may be retained. After that come drafting phone scripts (sometimes in multiple languages), call-handling training and recording a message for the call tree. A dedicated toll-free number should be assigned and a call escalation process identified. Other preparations may include:

- Creating, approving and uploading e-mail templates
- Training quality assurance team on the details of the initiative
- Pulling and analyzing reports
- Monitoring call levels to determine staffing needs

4.4.6 Remediation Offers

Besides trying to protect incident victims' identities, companies tend to offer remediation services to soften the blow of a breach. If a remediation offer is made, the organization should facilitate the dialog between the parties involved, which typically include the credit-monitoring provider, letter print shop and call center.

As a best practice, the notification letter should feature a full description of the remediation product, enrollment instructions, and a customer service phone number or e-mail address. An activation code, by which the recipient may redeem the remediation product, should also be included. To assure close collaboration between the three groups, the following steps are highly recommended.

Remediation Organization

- Create one activation code per affected person for inclusion in notification letters.
- Provide a full product description to the printer and the call center vendor, along with a toll-free number and an enrollment website URL.
- Launch and test the website for enrolments.
- Ramp up and train internal call center staff to enable phone enrollments and answering product questions.
- Approve the final letter copy as it pertains to the accuracy of the offer details.

Print Shop

- Obtain product description and activation codes from remediation firm.
- Merge product copy and activation codes into notification letters.
- Print and mail letters, according to agreed-upon standards and timelines.

Call Center

- Receive product description and, as appropriate, train internal staff on basic product questions.
- Determine and institute call transfer procedures between the vendor call center, remediation firm and affected organization.

4.5 Progress Reporting

During the breach response, the team leader is responsible for keeping all aspects of the initiative on track. If the leader is to accurately assess progress and identify potential trouble spots, functional leaders must provide timely, detailed reports at pre-determined intervals.

These intervals can vary greatly, depending on a breach's size and complexity. They should always be customized to each individual event. Similarly, the dynamics of the incident may influence how activities come into and out of different reporting timeframes. The appropriate authorities should be updated, as required by law; legal counsel can help decide how frequently these updates should be issued. Common reporting intervals include:

Hourly

Hourly updates are rare but still occasionally requested. In the period immediately following victim notification, for example, critical call center metrics may be reported hourly. Factors such as the number of calls received, average talk time and abandonment rates should be closely monitored to help adjust staffing levels. Long wait times, which can irritate and anger already confused or highly emotional callers, should be avoided.

Daily

Incident-response team meetings should be held daily, for at least a few weeks after an event. Groups should be updated about the day's challenges, status of targeted milestones and any subsequent or emerging objectives.

During the active notification period, mail drops should be reviewed at least daily to ensure alignment with approved delivery deadlines. Additionally, mailing and call center activities should be closely coordinated to ensure response staffing levels are optimal. In situations where victims receive credit-activity monitoring or other remediation, it may be beneficial to track enrollments and customer escalations daily for at least the first few weeks.

In the first days or weeks (depending on the severity of the incident), senior management should be briefed on the developments on a daily basis.

Often, the public relations group will track daily breach-related news coverage to confirm that the organization's event narrative is being interpreted as intended. To mitigate public backlash, clarifying responses to inaccuracies or negative press should be prepared and practiced in advance.

Weekly

Investors and other external stakeholders will naturally want to keep abreast of all breach-related developments. If the organization is publicly traded, senior management should be updated at least weekly for the first few months after breach notification.

Monthly

Regular reviews should be scheduled to update functional leaders, senior managers and other key stakeholders about the status and impact of the incident-response effort. A breach's effects on employee productivity and morale should not be underestimated, so keeping workers informed about how the incident is being handled is always a top priority.

4.6 Response Evaluation and Modifications

Once the initial chaos of a breach has subsided, the affected organization should carefully evaluate its incident-response plan. Even the most well thought-out responses can benefit from the lessons learned after a "live" event.

Among the most beneficial questions to answer about the response are:

- Which parts of the process clearly worked as intended?
- Which worked only after some modification?
- Which did not work at all?

- What did the team do exceptionally well? What didn't go well?
- Were any unforeseen complications encountered? How could they have been avoided?
- How well was the team prepared for the unexpected?
- How realistic were the plan's response timelines?
- What was the difference between actual and budgeted costs?
- Was the team sufficiently staffed?
- Were all relevant parties part of the team?
- What could be learned and what be improved for the next potential breach?

4.6.1 Calculating the Costs

While many breach-related costs can be identified and tallied using actual invoices, others are less apparent. Lost business opportunities and damage to brand equity are examples that may impact the bottom line for years following a breach. Table 7.1 includes typical categories of breach-related expenses in cases where costs can be traced to specific activities.

Table 7.1: Breach-Related Expenses

Expense	Description
Crisis Management/Public Relations	Experts to help the organization craft and deliver cohesive, properly timed and customer-friendly communications about the incident.
Forensic Investigators	Specialists to confirm, contain and eliminate the cause of the breach and also determine the size, scale and type of records affected.
Victim Notification	Creation and delivery of letters, e-mails, web pages and other methods/channels to notify affected individuals about the incident.
Call Center Support	Staffing, training and supporting the customer care team responsible for handling calls and e-mails related to the incident and its aftermath.
Outside Counsel	Legal review of the organization's contractual and regulatory obligations after a breach. May include defense costs if litigation results.
Equipment Replacement and Security Enhancements	Equipment changes, system upgrades and physical security improvements to mitigate the current breach and prevent future incidents.
Lost Revenue and Stock Value	Reductions in stock price, lost customers and other revenue decreases directly related to the loss.

Insurance	Retention (deductible) payments and fee increases associated with the breach.
Remediation Offers	Providing breach victims with services, such as credit monitoring, fraud resolution and identity theft insurance.
Punitive Costs	Fines, lawsuits and other penalties stemming from negligence in preventing or improperly responding to the breach.
Customer Retention	Marketing campaigns designed to prevent customer attrition and win back lost business following an incident.
Employee Training	Educational activities intended to improve upon previous programs that facilitated the compromise.
Card Replacement	In incidents when credit card numbers have been compromised, the affected organization may have to absorb the cost of issuing new cards.
Victim Damages	Costs related to correcting damages incurred by breach victims.
Opportunity Costs	Lost productivity and revenues, as employees suspend regularly assigned tasks to assist with breach response.

4.6.2 Cyber Liability Insurance

Insurance may be a viable funding source for helping to offset breach-response and recovery costs. While traditional policies may provide a certain level of protection, they do not normally cover expenses resulting from a data compromise. To reduce exposure, risk managers must work closely with insurance carriers and finance stakeholders to select the right type and level of coverage *prior* to an incident. A relatively new type of coverage called cyber liability insurance may cover many breach-related expenses, including:

- Forensic investigations
- Outside counsel fees
- Crisis management services
- Public relations experts
- Breach notification
- Call center costs
- Credit monitoring
- Fraud resolution services

5. Summary

The respond phase of the privacy operational life cycle provides guidance for managing information requests, meeting legal compliance, planning for incident response, and handling privacy incidents. An organization needs to be prepared to respond to its internal and external stakeholders—including regulators. The privacy professional and related team members need to be prepared to respond appropriately to each incoming request to reduce organizational risk and bolster compliance to regulations.

Endnotes

1   Ponemon Institute Research Report, "2011 Cost of Data Breach Study, United States: Benchmark Research Conducted by Ponemon Institute LLC" Report: March 2012.

2   OMB Memorandum M-07-16, "Safeguarding against and Responding to the Breach of Personally Identifiable Information" (May 22, 2007). www.whitehouse.gov/sites/default/files/omb/memoranda/fy2007/m07-16.pdf.

3   Canadian Privacy Commission, *Getting Accountability Right with a Privacy Management Program*, www.priv.gc.ca/information/guide/2012/gl_acc_201204_e.asp.

4   U.S. Department of Labor, Bureau of Labor Statistics, (2011). www.bls.gov/news.release/union2.nr0.htm.

5   www.aflcio.org/About/AFL-CIO-Unions.

6   Checkpoint Software Technologies, *The Risk of Social Engineering on Information Security: A Survey of IT Professionals,* September 2011. www.checkpoint.com/press/downloads/social-engineering-survey.pdf.

7   2011 AT&T Business Continuity Study.

8   Ponemon Institute, *Aftermath of a Data Breach,* (2012). www.experian.com/assets/data-breach/brochures/ponemon-aftermath-study.pdf.

9   European Commission, *Proposal for a Regulation of the European Parliament and of the Council* 29, January 25, 2012. http://ec.europa.eu/justice/data-protection/document/review2012/com_2012_11_en.pdf.

Index

Hong Kong Trade Development Council
(HKTDC), 5
human resources (HR), 96, 134, 165–166, 178,
182–183
hybrid governance, 20–21

I

IBM Corporation, 89–90
IEC (International Electrotechnical
Commission), 45–46
IFEA (Internet Free Expression Alliance), 48
ILM (information life cycle management),
105–110, 142
incident, defining, 173
incident detection
causes of breaches and reporting, 174–175
notification requirements and guidelines,
175–177
incident handling
incident response plan, 180–185
prenotification process, 179–180
incident management, 115
incident management and breach response
team, 98
incident planning and response, 163–178. *See
also* incident response plan
budgeting, 172–173
business continuity plan (BCP), 171–173
business development (BD) role in, 167
communications and PR role in, 167–168
customer care role in, 170–171
cyber liability insurance, 169, 191
execution timeline, 185–188
finance role in, 169
human resources (HR) role in, 165–166, 178
incident detection, 173–177
incident handling, 179–191
information security (IS) role in, 164
interdepartmental cooperation, 177–179
key roles and responsibilities, 163–171
legal stakeholder role in, 164–165
marketing role in, 166
physical security, 177–178
president, CEO role in, 169–170
progress reporting, 188–189
response evaluation and modification,
189–191

stakeholders and roles, 163–171
third-parties and security, 178
tools of prevention, 179
union role in, 168
incident response plan, 180–185
response team members, 181–185
team leader, 181
individual participation, 35
industry frameworks, 30, 49–50, 128
Information and Privacy Commissioner,
Ontario, Canada, 88
information governance, 106–107
information life cycle management (ILM),
105–110, 142
information requests, 153–157
corrections, 156
data integrity, 156–157
handling procedures, 154–155
organization accessibility, 155–156
redress, 156
information security (IS), 14, 94–95, 108,
110–121, 164
generic competency areas, 113–121
high-level security roles, 113
privacy vs. security, 112–113
risk management and, 110–111
information security management system
(ISMS), 45
information security triad, 112
information technology. *See* IT (information
technology)
infrastructure adequacy, 108
internal audits (IA), 15, 91–92, 138, 139–140, 141
internal awareness programs, 145
internal interfacing process, 15–16
internal monitoring, 134
internal partnerships, 11–13
internal policy compliance, 32–33
internal threats/vulnerabilities, 131
International Electrotechnical Commission
(IEC), 45–46
International Organization for Standardization
(ISO), 30, 45–46, 50
International Security, Trust, and Privacy
Alliance (ISTPA) framework, 50
Internet Free Expression Alliance (IFEA), 48
Internet Privacy Coalition (IPC), 48

About the Authors

Executive Editor

Russell R. Densmore, CIPP/US, CIPP/IT

Russell R. Densmore is the deputy chief privacy officer for Lockheed Martin Corporation. Densmore helped pioneer the corporate-wide privacy team at Lockheed Martin and has been instrumental in developing and implementing privacy practices and training across multiple business areas and functions.

Densmore has been involved in information technology engineering, information security, law enforcement and physical security for over 30 years. He has specialized in computer forensics, enterprise network security, investigations, and civil and criminal prosecutions and has been recognized by the U.S. Attorney General and the Federal Bureau of Investigation for support against cyber criminals.

Densmore received his BS in computer information systems from Regis University and is also a Certified Information Systems Security Professional (CISSP®) and Certified Forensic Analyst (CFA).

LOCKHEED MARTIN

We never forget who we're working for®

Lockheed Martin is a premier systems integrator and global security company principally engaged in the research, design, development, manufacture, integration and sustainment of advanced technology systems, products and services. With growth markets in defense, homeland security and systems/government information technology, Lockheed Martin delivers innovative technologies that help customers address complex challenges of strategic and national importance.

Headquartered in Bethesda, Maryland, Lockheed Martin employs 120,000 people worldwide. Lockheed Martin is led by Marillyn A. Hewson, Chief Executive Officer and President. Lockheed Martin's operating units are organized into five broad business areas with diverse lines of business: Aeronautics, Missiles and Fire Control, Mission Systems and Training, Space Systems and Information Systems and Global Solutions.

Distinguished by a passion for innovation and excellence in performance, Lockheed Martin has earned a reputation as the partner of choice, supplier of choice and employer of choice in the global marketplace. Governments worldwide are involved in meeting vital strategic goals to defend the peace, make their borders and homeland secure, or manage large information technology infrastructure projects. Lockheed Martin has more than 300 alliances, joint ventures and other partnerships in 75 countries.

The men and women of Lockheed Martin are committed to the highest standards of ethical business conduct and creating a sustainable future. Lockheed Martin also supports Science, Technology, Engineering and Math (STEM) education with initiatives such as Engineers in the Classroom and mentoring.

Contributors

James M. Byrne, CIPP/US, CIPP/G, CIPP/IT

James M. Byrne is chief privacy officer and associate general counsel for Lockheed Martin Corporation. As the corporation's CPO, Byrne oversees all activities related to the development, implementation, maintenance and adherence to the organization's policies and procedures covering the privacy of employee and program data in compliance with federal, state, local and international privacy laws, regulations and program requirements. He is also responsible as an associate general counsel for enterprise records management and electronic discovery and previously managed a domestic and international ethics and business conduct program for the company.

Before joining Lockheed Martin, Byrne was a career senior executive service official with over 20 years of professional experience in the military and federal government, including several years as a U.S. Department of Justice international narcotics prosecutor and deployed U.S. Marine Corps infantry officer. Prior to leaving the government Byrne served as the deputy special counsel with the Office of the U.S. Special Counsel. He also served overseas with the Office of the Special Inspector General for Iraq reconstruction. Soon after the invasion of Iraq in 2003, Byrne returned to active duty for 18 months with the Marine Corps in support of the Global War on Terrorism. Byrne serves on the Board of Directors for the IAPP and in May 2012 was appointed by the Secretary of the U.S. Department of Homeland Security to serve on the Data Protection and Integrity Advisory Board. He is a graduate of the U.S. Naval Academy and Stetson University College of Law.

Elisa Choi, CIPP/IT

Elisa Choi is a manager within Ernst & Young's Privacy Advisory Services practice through which she serves the firm's leading global and domestic clients. Choi is responsible for providing clients with an array of privacy and data protection-related services including the development of corporate privacy governance and compliance functions, creation of privacy policies and procedures, enterprise privacy assessments and privacy incident management and triage support. She has also worked with a number of companies in the areas of HIPAA Privacy and Security, U.S. Department of Commerce Safe Harbor Privacy Program certification/recertification and compliance with the EU Data Protection Directive. In addition to her involvement in the privacy arena, Choi's experience in the advisory space includes IT compliance audits under the Sarbanes-Oxley 404 framework, system implementation reviews around technical infrastructure and business processes and security compliance audit evaluations. Choi has worked with numerous U.S. and global Fortune 500 businesses and has gained experience in the pharmaceutical, health services, consumer and commercial electronics, retail manufacturing and sales, aerospace and defense and financial services industries.

In addition to Choi's client serving responsibilities, she is actively involved in Ernst & Young's thought leadership. She has been an active contributor in the ongoing development of the firm's global privacy methodology, which focuses on incorporating industry-leading practices while delivering consistent, high-quality privacy solutions to clients.

Choi earned bachelor of business administration (BBA) and master of science in information systems technology (MS-IST) degrees from The George Washington University in Washington, DC. She is an active member of the IAPP and several other professional organizations including the Information Systems Audit and Control Association (ISACA).

ᆲ ERNST & YOUNG
Quality In Everything We Do

Ernst & Young is a global leader in assurance, tax, transaction and advisory services. Worldwide, our 167,000 people are united by our shared values and an unwavering commitment to quality. We make a difference by helping our people, our clients and our wider communities achieve their potential.

Ernst & Young refers to the global organization of member firms of Ernst & Young Global Limited, each of which is a separate legal entity. Ernst & Young Global Limited, a UK company limited by guarantee, does not provide services to clients. For more information about our organization, please visit www.ey.com.

Ozzie Fonseca, CIPP/US
Ozzie Fonseca is a senior director for Experian's Data Breach Resolution Group and has been involved in the identity protection arena for nearly a decade. Fonseca is a frequent speaker on data breach preparedness and incident response, and he is a regular blogger for Experian.com/DBBlog.

In his role at Experian, Fonseca has helped thousands of organizations of every size, and virtually in every industry, respond to data compromises affecting from hundreds to millions of victims. During his tenure in the privacy industry, Fonseca has earned a strong reputation as a trusted advisor and a key asset when addressing data breaches. He consistently brings to the table his extensive practical experience in handling large scale breach notifications, setting up incident response call centers and providing best-in-class identity protection and fraud resolution services.

Fonseca has also served on the IAPP's Educational Advisory Board.

Before his involvement in the world of privacy, Fonseca spent most of his career as an educator in the auto insurance, telecom and credit industries responsible for developing training programs across the corporate spectrum.

Fonseca holds bachelor's and master's degrees in business administration.

Experian® is a leader in the data breach resolution industry and one of the first companies to develop services that address this critical issue. Experian has a long-standing history of providing swift and effective data breach resolution for thousands of organizations, having serviced millions of affected consumers. Experian Data Breach Resolution services enable organizations to plan for and successfully respond to data breaches. Learn more at http://www.experian.com/databreach.

Edward P. Yakabovicz, CIPP/IT

As a principal engineer for the Center for Cyber Security Innovation at Lockheed Martin Corporation, Edward P. Yakabovicz has over 30 years of business experience architecting security designs for worldwide global networks and implementing highly detailed security solutions for the top five financial corporations, the U.S. government, local U.S. state governments and Lockheed Martin global customers.

As a subject matter expert in cybersecurity and privacy, Yakabovicz has managed and consulted on computer network defense, computer incident response, security architectures, certification and accreditation, and information technology systems management.

Yakabovicz holds a master's degree in information assurance from Norwich University in Vermont and is currently a PhD student in information assurance at Capitol College in Maryland. He also holds several certifications, including the (ISC)² Certified Information Systems Security Professional (CISSP®).

Yakabovicz dedicates his work in this book to his family, Lockheed Martin colleagues, and all the people around the globe that provide friendship, mentoring, support and guidance for this effort and the advancement to privacy and security knowledge.

Amy E. Yates, CIPP/US

Amy E. Yates is the chief privacy officer of Avanade Inc., a provider of business technology solutions and managed services. Yates served as the acting privacy officer of Andersen in 2001, and went on to become the first chief privacy officer of Hewitt Associates (now Aon Hewitt) until 2007. She has also delivered data protection and security services as a member of several global consulting and law firms. Yates served on the IAPP Board of Directors and is a frequent speaker on privacy and data protection issues.

Yates graduated from Georgetown University, School of Foreign Service with an emphasis on Chinese and Asian Studies, thereafter attending Taiwan Political University for two years. She received her law degree from Northwestern University School of Law.

Avanade provides business technology solutions and managed services that connect insight, innovation and expertise in Microsoft technologies to help customers realize results. Our people have helped thousands of organizations in all industries improve business agility, employee productivity, and customer loyalty. Avanade combines the collective business, technical and industry expertise of its worldwide network of experts with the rigor of an industrialized delivery model to provide high quality solutions using proven and emerging technologies with flexible deployment models—on premises, cloud-based or outsourced. Avanade, which is majority owned by Accenture, was founded in 2000 by Accenture LLP and Microsoft Corporation and has 17,000 professionals in more than 20 countries. Additional information can be found at www.avanade.com.

PRIV PROG MGMNT